RUST TO RENEWAL

WHY CHURCHES MUST WORK TOGETHER TO LEAD ECONOMIC AND SOCIAL TRANSFORMATION IN YOUNGSTOWN, OHIO

JOSHUA D. REICHARD

FORWARD BY DAVID L. THOMAS

VISION PUBLISHING
Ramona, California U.S.A.

© Copyright 2007 by Joshua D. Reichard.

All rights reserved. For permission to reuse content, please contact Copyright Clearance Center, 222 Rosewood Drive, Danvers MA, 01923, (978) 750-8400, www.thenewcopyright.com

Included images and illustrations used are free of copyright to the knowledge of the author and publisher.

ISBN # 1-931178-13-5

Visit Rust to Renewal on the World Wide Web at:
www.rusttorenewal.com

Visit Vision Publishing on the World Wide Web at
www.visionpublishingservices.com

Printed in the United States of America.

Dedicated to:

The hard working families of Youngstown, Ohio, and the dedicated clergy from every church that maintains hope for the city's economic future.

Table of Contents

Forward by David L. Thomas	9
Author's Preface	11

CHAPTER 1:
Introduction: The Tofflerian Socioeconomic Wave Model 15
   Alvin Toffler and the Third Wave 15
   Religious Attitudes and Tofflerian Socioeconomic Model 16
   What makes Youngstown, Ohio unique? 18
   Some Background Information 19
   The Research Contained in this Book 23
   Research Significance 23
   A Theoretical Framework for understanding Social and
      Economic Change 24
   Summary of the Research Approach 24
   How the Research was Conducted 29

CHAPTER 2: Second Wave Economics in Youngstown 33
   The Industrial Revolution 33
   The Second Wave and the Youngstown Steel Crisis of 1977 35
     Second Wave Religious Attitudes and Deindustrialization 37
     Second Wave Religious Attitudes: Community focused 41
     Second Wave Religious Attitudes: Justice-Oriented 44
     Second Wave Religious Attitudes: Activism-oriented 46
   The Prominence of Mainline Protestantism and
      Roman Catholicism at the End of the Second Wave 48
   The Ecumenical Coalition of the Mahoning Valley 50

CHAPTER 3: Third Wave Economics in Youngstown 57
   The Third Wave and Demassified Technology 57
   Third Wave Industry and Youngstown Manufacturing 60
   National Trends and Manufacturing Labor Decline 66
   National Trends and Globalization 69
   The Third Wave and Downsized Ohio Labor 72

CHAPTER 4:
Third Wave Religious Attitudes in Youngstown 77
   Third Wave Religious Attitudes and Deindustrialization 77
   The Prominence of Evangelicalism 79
      Third Wave Religious Attitudes: Individuality-Focused 82
      Third Wave Religious Attitudes: Charity-Oriented 84
      Third Wave Religious Attitudes: Piety-Oriented 88
   Summary of Third Wave Religious Attitudes 90

CHAPTER 5: Research Findings 95
   An Important Note to the Reader 95
   Research Hypotheses 95
   How the Data was Collected 98
   Denominational Representation 99
   Research Findings Summary 100
   Hypothesis Analyses Summary 101

CHAPTER 6: Interpretation of the Research 103
   Conclusions 105
      Second and Third Wave Socio-economic Values and
         denominational affiliation 105
      Third Wave Values and blue collar and white collar
         congregations 106
      Justice Values and denominational affiliation 106
      Justice Values and blue collar and white collar congregations 107
      Justice Values among those who participated in the
         Ecumenical Coalition of 1977 and those who did not 107
      Justice Values among urban, suburban, and rural
         congregations 108
      Charity Values among those who participated in the
         Ecumenical Coalition of 1977 and those who did not 108
      Charity Values among clergy representing congregations
         that have financially supported workers affected by
         downsizing and those that have not 109
      Charity Values among urban, suburban, and rural
         congregations 109
      Piety Values and denominational affiliation 109
      Activism Values and denominational affiliation 110
      Activism Values among those who participated in the
         Ecumenical Coalition of 1977 and those who did not 110
      Community Values and denominational affiliation 111
      Individuality Values and denominational affiliation 111
   Implications of the Research 112
      Future Research 116
      Summary of Research Findings 116

CHAPTER 7: Conclusion
The Fourth Wave and Transformational Christianity   119
    An Integrative Social Theology   119
    Transformational Christianity   123
        A Statement from the Lausanne Covenant   125
        Missional Living   127
        Marketplace Ministry   130
        The Church of the Locality   132
        A Model for Transformational Christianity   134
    Conclusion: Application and Action   138
    Survey Utilized by the Research   143

Bibliography   149
Works Cited   151
Related Works   161
Index   165

Forward by David L. Thomas
Senior Pastor, Victory Christian Center

To the Reader:

When I graduated from High School in 1970, I had a number of viable options: employment at General Motors Lordstown, Delphi (then know simply as Packard Electric), one of the booming steel mills, or post-secondary education. On my nineteenth birthday, August 7th, 1970, I was hired at General Motors Lordstown. I wore my General Motors badge with pride. Four years and three months later I took a great step of faith and forfeited my secure job at General Motors to enter vocational ministry. For nearly thirty years, I have since served as Senior Pastor at Victory Christian Center. I now oversee three campuses, several partner churches, and over five thousand congregants.

"Rust to Renewal" chronicles the deindustrialization of Youngstown as well as the valiant attempts by religious leaders to save the jobs lost on Black Monday in 1977. Although I have lived in Youngstown my entire life and thought I was well-educated regarding our local economy, my eyes were certainly opened to many significant details that I never before encountered. The book you are about to read provides an eye-opening glimpse of Youngstown's past and a message of hope for Youngstown's future. As I have traveled a good part of the world, I have not found any harder working or honest people than those of the greater Youngstown area. I believe in this area and its people!

"As he (a person) thinks in his heart, so is he..."
--- Proverbs 23:7a

One of Youngstown's great challenges is a change in our thinking. We must be creative and proactive to secure our economic future. We must realize that although the old days are never coming back, we can become more solution oriented together. Our destiny will not be found in our past, but in our future. Thank God for the legacy left by many hard working, family-oriented men and women who have called Youngstown home, but may we as a community set our sights on the infinite possibilities of the future.

We must work together, all Christians, all churches, and all people, to see the transformation that Dr. Reichard proclaims. Be certain not just to glance at the well gathered statistics and data, but meditate upon the solutions that "Rust to Renewal" presents. If we cooperate with one another for the common good of the Youngstown area we will perhaps better realize John Wesley's understanding that:

"Without God we cannot, but without us God will not."

Together for transformation,

The Reverend David L. Thomas
Senior Pastor, Victory Christian Center
President, Next Level Leadership Network

Author's Preface

To the Reader:

This book was derived from research I conducted for my doctoral dissertation. Much of the statistical and social scientific details have been removed for purposes of the reception of a broader audience. For those who are interested in the details of the research, the original dissertation is available via University Microfilm/UMI dissertation abstracts.

I pursued the research direction herein after encountering two books: Alvin Toffler's *The Third Wave* and Thomas Feuchtmann's *Steeples and Stacks*. Coincidentally, I was scheduled to graduate in 2007, exactly 30 years following the Youngstown Steel Crisis of 1977 and the Ecumenical Coalition that formed in response. I saw this as a unique opportunity to contribute original research and a fresh perspective on the economic crises faced by Youngstown in 2007 and in the future.

I trust that this book will influence the future of Youngstown and will, in some small way, contribute to genuine social and economic transformation that translates into religious response, real jobs, innovative industry, corporate reform, and political action. I also hope that this book serves as a looking glass for the clergy of Youngstown, that we may not only be self-reflective enough to admit our theological and practical weaknesses, but that we may also come to appreciate the strengths of our brothers and sisters with whom we may not see eye-to-eye. The goal of this book is to move beyond exclusivity and ecumenism to a new era of committed cooperation with a principal mission guiding and uniting us: *to see Youngstown transformed.*

Together, I believe this goal is achievable.

Sincerely,

Dr. Joshua Reichard
2007

Special Thanks

Special thanks to Brian Corbin of the Catholic Diocese of Youngstown, Dr. John Russo of the Center for Working Class Studies at Youngstown State University, and the faculty of The Oxford Graduate School American Centre for Religion and Society Studies, without whom the research herein would have been impossible.

Rust to Renewal

CHAPTER 1

Introduction: The Tofflerian Socioeconomic Wave Model

Alvin Toffler and the Third Wave

In 1970 futurist Alvin Toffler predicted a shift in developed nations from industrial societies to information societies. Toffler (1989) described societies in three basic stages: *First*, *Second*, and *Third* wave societies. The waves, as Toffler described them, pushed preceding societies aside to make room for social and economic progress. Toffler's model provided a metaphor of human history, demonstrating the social evolution of humanity from a primitive hunter-gatherer society, to an agricultural (First Wave), to an industrial (Second Wave), and to a postindustrial technological society (Third Wave). Toffler's economic wave model and the trends of the Third Wave in particular were confirmed by other futurists, including Drucker (1950, 1989) and Naisbitt (1982).

First Wave societies (also known as primary sectors), were agrarian societies where land ownership and the production and trade of agricultural goods dictated the success of the economy. Second Wave societies (secondary sectors) were industrial economies where factory labor, manpower, and mass production dictated economic success. Third Wave societies (tertiary and quaternary sectors), according to Toffler, were information societies where technology, data, and knowledge were paramount to the outmoded forms of Second Wave industrialism. The critical driving force of economic growth in the Third Wave was not the super normal profits that technological change generated but the continuous creation of opportunities for perpetual technological development (Carlaw & Lispey, 2003). The Third Wave, according to Toffler, was the wave of continual technological progress that eclipsed the industrialism of the Second Wave.

Alvin Toffler (c. 1990)   The Third Wave (1980)

Religious Attitudes and Tofflerian Socioeconomic Model

Philips (2006) recognized that change in theological dominance tended to be the harbinger of broader political and social change (Philips, 2006). Religion has a generative social power and its influence historically affects social values. Economic issues relevant to industrialization and deindustrialization were present in American religious life since the inception of the country and just as Toffler's model of society and economics was represented in waves, religion as a social institution underwent corresponding transitions. As the economy and society in America changed, religion changed, adapting to the needs and ideologies of communities and individuals.

Religion has significantly contributed to the American understanding of the nature of work, wealth, and social responsibility. As Novak (1981) noted, there was hardly a less well-developed area in the tradition of Christian thought than the relation of Christianity to economics. Historically, religious traditions and movements displayed remarkably distinct patterns of both withdrawal from and engagement with American public life as social and economic progress occurred (Regnerus & Smith, 1998). Although the economic attitudes of religious leaders did not always translate into action by local congregations, such attitudes represented the initiative of sufficiently concerned individuals toward ethical social change (Feuchtman, 1988). Whether the influence of religion on economics was positive or negative, it is an historical and contemporary reality that must be engaged. Toffler's socioeconomic wave model is representative of shifting religious attitudes toward deindustrialization and can be used to better understand the evolution of religious thought during America's economic transition.

What makes Youngstown, Ohio unique?

As predicted by Toffler (1981), the American economy is in transition from an industrial economy to an information economy. The city of Youngstown, part of the "rustbelt" of the Northeastern United States, is a symbol of American postindustrial economic blight. The skyline of Youngstown is littered with the rusting smokestacks of steel mills that have been out of operation for three or four decades. The economic depression of Youngstown is apparent as government housing projects, empty lots, and urban ruin comprise the city's low-end real estate market in the shadow of a once booming industrial economy. According to the Tofflerian socioeconomic wave model, Youngstown, like America as a whole, is slowly shifting from Second Wave industrialism to a Third Wave technology and service economy.

In 2007 and beyond, the greater Youngstown area of the Mahoning Valley faces new crises similar to the steel crises of the 1970s. Area automobile and product manufacturers are outsourcing labor to developing nations as the surviving Youngstown area industries struggle to enter the Third Wave economy of globalization and technology, as Toffler predicted.

The local economy of Youngstown and the surrounding area, the Mahoning Valley, continue to decline as the city deindustrializes from a once booming steel economy. While the economic blight is not atypical for a rust belt steel town, religious involvement sets Youngstown apart. When Youngstown steel mills closed in 1977, the city attracted national attention for the unusual support the area religious community rallied to save the steel industry. Although the religious response of the 1970s was largely considered a failure, it set Youngstown in stark contrast to other rustbelt cities that underwent similar transitions. Now, 30 years since the steel crises and the peculiar religious response that followed, the churches of the Youngstown area must reflect on the past and discover new and creative ways to bring about social and economic recovery.

Some Background Information

Religion and economics are not unfamiliar acquaintances in Youngstown. When steel mills closed in the 1970s, the religious community was outspoken and socially active in an unparalleled attempt to save the steel industry from demise. Although the religious community of Youngstown was unsuccessful in its efforts to change the economic collapse of the steel industry, their participation in the crisis caused Youngstown national attention while dozens of other rust belt cities quietly suffered the same economic collapse. Nevertheless, the responses of the religious community of Youngstown were characteristic of Toffler's Second Wave socioreligious patterns and concerns and in step with his futuristic predictions.

Beyond 2007 Youngstown will undergoing another economic shift as area manufacturers downsize the labor force and administer mass layoffs. Unlike the 1970s, the religious community is not rallying a public response. The religious community is either not reacting to present labor crises or is reacting in a more subtle, nonpublic manner. As the economy changes, a religious response is necessary to care for the thousands of families of displaced workers, to cope with the rippling effects on the local economy, and to provide perspective for the consequences of the future. As the economy of the Mahoning Valley continues to deindustrialize and transition out of the manufacturing sector, the clergy and religious communities are obligated to respond to the socioeconomic crises the transition initiates.

Struggles between labor unions and management are consistent as laborers strive to save their jobs and benefits, while management strives to save companies that cannot compete with less expensive foreign labor. There will be a temporary economic crisis as midcareer baby-boomer laborers, who have no post-secondary education or technical skills, are downsized from labor positions held for twenty or more years. In the face of such downsizing, midcareer transitional workers will be forced either to be retrained for new careers or to seek service employment at a significantly lower-wage. In economies such as Youngstown, where workers rely on unskilled manufacturing labor positions to maintain a middle-class standard of living, the effects will be devastating to the entire community during this transitional period. As it was during periods of transition in the past, the religious community must play a part in Youngstown's socioeconomic evolution.

Social concern for economic issues is historically interwoven with the mission of most religious denominations and movements in the Christian tradition. In like manner, social concern for economic issues was historically expressed by the religious communities of Youngstown. As the city faces new economic challenges

30 years after the social activism of the 1970s, such concern is not as public. Unlike the 1970s steel crisis, religious communities are not outspoken about the economic crises: it is rare to find social commentary on the situation by the Youngstown area clergy in television, radio, or print. Religious communities may have learned from the sour experiences of the past and elected to abstain from public social involvement in the current economic crises, addressing issues quietly to avoid politicization. Nevertheless, religious leaders have not voiced a strong public opinion or taken noticeable public social action.

Causes of the lack of a religious response in to the labor crises in Youngstown are characteristic of Toffler's Third Wave social trends: (a) suburbanization of religion and the labor force, (b) the transformation of the American economy from a labor market to a service and information market, and (c) the political mobilization of Evangelical Christianity. The city of Youngstown, the United States, and the world have changed significantly since the 1970s, and as societies changed, religion has also changed. Second Wave religion was supplanted by Third Wave religion.

As the economy of the developed world transitions from the Second Wave to the Third Wave, Youngstown can serve as a benchmark of religious concern for similar economic transitions in postindustrial urban communities worldwide. The attitudes of clergy toward the problem are a small indication of how the responses of religious communities in the Youngstown area changed since the 1970s. The attitudes of clergy demonstrate whether religious communities accept or reject the difficult transition out of an industrial age and into an information age as predicted by futurists and economists such as Toffler.

In perspective with national and global economic shifts, economic and sociological data indicate that labor crises in areas similar to Youngstown are temporary, localized, and small-scale as the national economy continues a transition from a predominantly industrial society to a predominantly technological society. Youngstown has lagged in its economic evolution and perpetually aligned with the side of issues that lead to further economic decline, job loss, poverty, and crime; all of which now characterize the city and directly affect and engage religious communities. Transition out of Toffler's Second Wave was unnecessarily difficult for Youngstown.

Although the manufacturing crises will be temporary, thousands of primary family incomes in a local community will be swiftly eliminated and the community as a whole will suffer. A social response to the labor crises from the churches and clergy is imperative, though such a response must differ from the less effective social activism of the 1970s that divided the community and ultimately impeded economic growth. If Youngstown area clergy learned from past failures, a more informed social response to the crises will potentially produce more positive long-term results for the community. An effective religious response to the crises will alleviate the difficulty of the transition into the Third Wave for thousands of displaced workers and the communities in which they live.

The Research Contained in this Book

Original sociological research was conducted to determine the attitudes of clergy in the Youngstown area toward the Third Wave manufacturing crises of beyond 2007 in comparison with the Second Wave labor crises of the 1970s. The research identified shifts in the attitudes of clergy toward the nature of the problem, the appropriate religious response, and the changing economic landscape of the Third Wave. It must be understood that social research can be ambiguous, descriptive, and only quasi-experimental. Social research is never conclusive and because its subjects are people in the real world, there is always a margin of error. However, the research that was conducted and the results that were computed will shed some light on the state of religion and economics in the Youngstown area.

Research Significance

The research in this book contributes to the ongoing struggle of confronting labor crises in a transitional economy faced by Youngstown, Ohio and other rustbelt cities. The research investigated the similarities and differences between the religious attitudes toward the steel crisis of the 1970s and the labor crises of the present and the future. The research probed attitudes of clergy, who were primarily uninvolved in the religious response of the 1970s, toward the new labor crises.

The research is intended to inform the religious community, parishioners and clergy alike, of attitudes toward the labor crises, which may potentially lead to a more collective and effective response to alleviate the effects of the crisis faced by the Youngstown community. The research will potentially lead to a more proactive public response of the clergy and religious communities, which may positively impact public policy, corporate business practices, and individual conduct.

The results of the research contained in this book are intended to be a small step in the direction of such enormous changes. Together, change, recovery, and renewal are possible.

A Theoretical Framework for understanding Social and Economic Change

All good research is grounded in theory. A theoretical framework is a guiding map by which research is conducted, or a lens through which research is analyzed. In order for the research into Youngstown's religious communities to be successful, a theoretical framework had to be employed that spoke to both social and economic trends. Thus, Alvin Toffler's socioeconomic wave model was selected.

A theoretical framework was established, based on a review of related literature, through which the relationships between religion and the labor crises of Youngstown was attitudinally assessed. The framework was based on several premises and derived from historic works concerning religious perspectives on economics, historic denominational attitudes, the socioeconomic transitions of labor and manufacturing, and the implications of globalization. The framework was based on placing religious attitudes toward deindustrialization and economic issues into the context of Toffler's socioeconomic wave model. The framework categorized religious attitudes toward socioeconomic problems in the context of Toffler's Second and Third Wave societies and demonstrated that the attitudes of the most prominent denominational structures were characteristic of the society in general during each corresponding social wave.

The framework identified two primary scales by which clergy attitudes would be assessed: Second Wave attitudes and Third Wave attitudes. Each scale was divided into three subscale attitudinal characteristics. The Second Wave attitudinal characteristics included: *value of community*, *value of justice*, and *value of activism*. The Third Wave attitudinal characteristics included: *value of individualism*, *value of charity*, and *value of piety*. The attitudinal characteristics were associated with the predominant religions in society during each wave. The Second Wave society was predominantly composed of and influenced by Mainline Protestants and Roman Catholics, whereas the Third Wave was predominantly composed of and influenced by Evangelicals and Fundamentalists.

Second and Third Wave divisions were determined based on denominational affiliation with the Ecumenical Coalition of the Mahoning Valley. The Ecumenical Coalition of the Mahoning Valley was the religious response group that acted in an attempt to save the steel mills from the 1977 shutdown. The Coalition will be discussed in greater detail and in proper context.

THEORETICAL FRAMEWORK OF THE INSTRUMENT		
will assess the attitudes of the Clergy toward		
SECOND WAVE ATTITUDES Preserving the Second Wave Industry		THIRD WAVE ATTITUDES Accepting the Third Wave Industrial Changes
Subscale:		Subscale:
Concern for Justice for Downsized Labor	vs.	Concern for Charity for Downsized Labor
Concern for Institutional/Social Activism	vs.	Concern for Personal Piety
Concern for Community	vs.	Concern for Individuality
To Determine		
How do clergy attitudes toward deindustrialization differ between denominations that were involved in the 1977 Youngstown steel crisis and those that remained uninvolved?		

Theoretical Framework of Variables Assessed by the Research

The following chart helps explain the differences between the Second and Third Wave, religiously, socially, and economically. The chart helps set into perspective the theory upon which the research was conducted and by which it can be interpreted. A clear understanding of Toffler's theory is beneficial to anyone who is concerned about deindustrialization in general and Youngstown's future in particular. The table below is merely theoretical and does not necessarily represent actualities in the Youngstown area. The broad generalizations represent general characteristics derived from the literature, applied to Youngstown's past and present situations.

Second Wave (Secondary Sector) Prior to 1977 Steel Crisis	Third Wave (Tertiary and Quaternary Sectors) 2007 Manufacturing Crisis	Mainline Protestant Roman Catholic	Evangelical Fundamentalist
Characteristics of Society/Economy		**Characteristics of Society/Religion**	
Industrial	Technological/Informational	Emphasis on Social Justice	Emphasis on Personal Charity
Massified Society	De-Massified Society	Emphasis on Activism	Emphasis on Piety
Urban Manufacturing	Suburban Service Economy	Urban Ethnic Churches	Suburban Multicultural Churches
Unions/Collective Bargaining	Individualized Workforce	Concern for Public Morality	Concern for Personal Morality
Nationalism	Globalization	Denominational religion	Free Market religion
Production-driven	Consumption-driven	Missiological	Apocalyptic
Characteristics of the Laborer		**Characteristics of the Clergy**	
1977 Steel Crisis	*2007 Manufacturing Crisis*	*Predominant during 1977 Steel Crisis*	*Predominant during 2007 Manufacturing Crisis*
Little forewarning of plant shutdown	Decades of forewarning of outsourcing and globalization	Concerned with long-term effects of plant closings and displaced workers	Concerned with immediate personal needs of displaced workers and their families

Table Continued			
Second Wave (Secondary Sector) Prior to 1977 Steel Crisis	Third Wave (Tertiary and Quaternary Sectors) 2007 Manufacturing Crisis	Mainline Protestant Roman Catholic	Evangelical Fundamentalist
Characteristics of Society/Economy		Characteristics of Society/Religion	
Characteristics of the Laborer		Characteristics of the Clergy	
Steel industry was still a significant part of economy	Manufacturing industry an insignificant part of economy	Concerned for fair treatment of displaced workers by companies	Concerned for charitable treatment of workers by churches
Only vested pensions available after job loss	Lump-sum buyout offers, retirement plans and pensions	Characterized by the Social Gospel and Catholic Social Teaching	Characterized by individualistic religion

Overview of society, economics, and religion in the Second and Third Waves

Summary of the Research Approach

The original research in this book investigated how the attitudes of Youngstown clergy toward deindustrialization in 2007 differed between denominations affiliated with the 1977 Ecumenical Coalition of the Mahoning Valley and denominations that were unaffiliated with the with the 1977 Ecumenical Coalition of the Mahoning Valley. The research, built upon the theoretical framework of the Tofflerian socioeconomic wave model, was designed to investigate clergy attitudes in relation to the economic decline precipitated by deindustrialization in Youngstown. Eight research hypotheses and seven corollary hypotheses were developed and tested. The results are helpful to everyone who lives and works in Youngstown, and especially self-revealing for the religious community.

Do not get lost in the technical details of the research. Look past the details and focus on the goal: to understand the social, economic, and religious situation in which Youngstown finds itself, and make changes for the future that will bring recovery and transformation. The information contained below simply describes how the research was conducted for those interested in the process.

How the Research was conducted

Some assumptions were made regarding the research. The research assumed that all participants were familiar with the manufacturing downsizing crisis of 2007. The crisis was well reported by newspapers and television stations in the Youngstown area. The research assumed that the participants answered the questions on the survey that was utilized (see appendix) with honesty and accuracy.

The research was limited to the assessment of attitudes of clergy in the Youngstown, Ohio/Mahoning Valley geographical area. Even though the research was particular to the geographical area of the Mahoning Valley, some practical value may be applicable to other rustbelt cities of similar population, economic condition, and labor market viability. Because of the unique involvement of the religious community in the 1977 steel crisis, some religious data produced by the research may not be applicable to other populations.

The research assessed attitudes of the clergy toward the deindustrialization of Youngstown and the present manufacturing crises faced by the Mahoning Valley. The research did not assess attitudes of past labor crises. Assumptions were made concerning the dominant views of past crises, informed by the review of literature.

The research was applicable for the brief period in which the manufacturing crises of 2007 were occurring. As demonstrated by a review of literature, the manufacturing crises were expected to be temporary and localized. The research was not repeatable in future situations without significant modification. The research was representative of clergy contained within a selected population.

The research was quantitative and utilized a modified grounded theory model. The research assessed the extension of Alvin Toffler's socioeconomic wave theory into the context of religion. The review of literature synthesized similarities between religious and economic trends in America to establish a theoretical framework by which the instrument was developed and the research was conducted.

The research utilized a Static Group Comparison Design. The samples were dichotomized from the population into two groups, based on the specific response to denominational affiliation on the survey. The unaffiliated group consisted of clergy from denominations that were unaffiliated with the Ecumenical Coalition of the Mahoning Valley in 1977 and the affiliated group consisted of denominations that were affiliated with the Ecumenical Coalition of the Mahoning Valley in 1977. The unaffiliated group consisted of all Evangelical, Fundamentalist, and other denominations that remained unaffiliated with the coalition in 1977. The affiliated group included all churches belonging to Roman Catholic and Mainline Protestant denominations that participated in the Ecumenical Coalition of the Mahoning Valley during the 1977 Youngstown steel crisis. The denominations included: The United Methodist Church, The Christian Church (Disciples of Christ), The United Church of Christ, The Episcopal Church, The Presbyterian Church USA, American Baptist, The Roman Catholic Church, and the Lutheran Church (ELCA and LCMS). Even though the Ecumenical Coalition included Eastern Orthodox and Jewish congregations, they were not considered in the Literature Review and were therefore excluded from the population of the research.

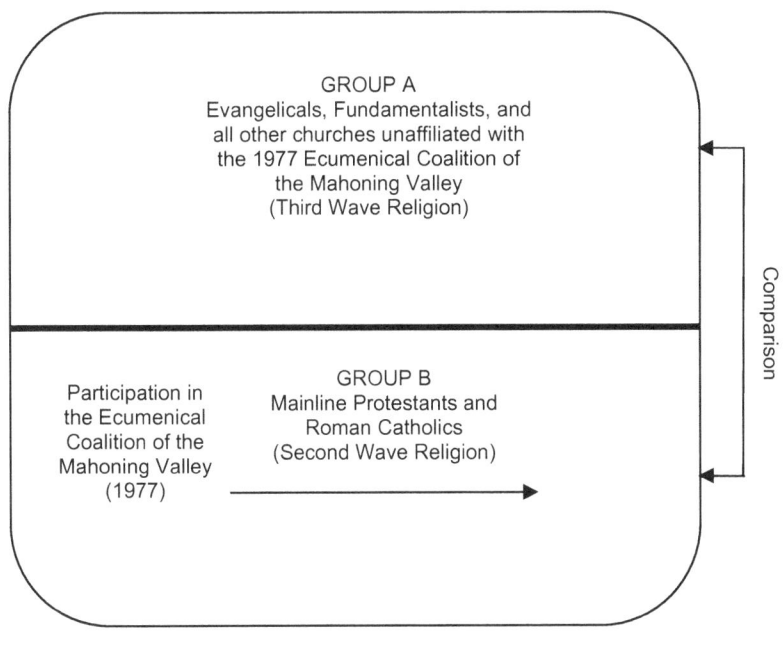

Research Design

CHAPTER 2
Second Wave Economics in Youngstown

The Industrial Revolution

In 1860 at the helm of the Industrial Revolution farming comprised approximately 50% of American jobs. In 1997, farming comprised only 3% of American jobs (Rowthorn & Ramaswamy, 1997), and the number is undoubtedly lower today. The First Wave of agrarian society is a long forgotten memory in the minds of Americans.

Productivity improvements in farming caused the shift from American agricultural economics to an industrialized economy. Toffler (1994) noted that at the advent of the Second Wave, "…masses of peasants were forced off the land to provide workers for the new 'satanic mills' and factories multiplied over the landscape" (Toffler, 2004, p.29). Factory labor increased and in 1892, when the Homestead Act was repealed and western agricultural expansion ended, the United States began to grow by urbanization and industrialization (Stackhouse, 1984). The Second Wave was on the horizon.

The Second Wave was characterized by the Industrial Revolution that began in the late eighteenth century and perpetuated after the American Civil War. In the Second Wave people left the peasant culture of farming to work in urban factories. Americans were dependent upon food, goods, or services produced by someone other than themselves; industrialism caused vast populations to migrate in search of jobs. Large populations were compressed into booming industrial centers (Toffler, 1980). Society became massified in its work, commerce, transportation, and media. Toffler (1980) asserted that the Second Wave promoted broad social massification by centralization and standardization. People were condensed into ethnical, cultural, religious, and vocational groups.

In the Second Wave economics moved from a peripheral position to the center of American life. Toffler (1980) noted that the "… explosive expansion of the market contributed to the fastest rise in living standards the world had ever experienced" (Toffler, 1980, p.40). With industrialization came the rapid prosperity of the American economy and the despair of the Great Depression. The Second Wave culminated in the Second World War: an explosion of "smokestacks, superpowers, and the atomic bomb".

Youngstown, like most rustbelt cities, clung to the principles of the Second Wave. Both the ideologies that made the Second Wave economically viable and those that ultimately made the Second Wave obsolete were characteristic of the economy and social structures of

Youngstown. Youngstown was a textbook Second Wave city.

West Federal Street, Youngstown, 1905.

The Second Wave and the Youngstown Steel Crisis of 1977

The local economy of Youngstown, Ohio was once dominated by steel mills and the entire local economy depended on steel (Fuechtmann, 1989). Buss (1983) noted that "Youngstown's steel workers were one of the most productive, best-paid, and seemingly secure industrial labor forces in the world" (p. 2). The population of Youngstown increased in the first two decades of the twentieth century, rising from 44,885 to 132,358 between 1900 and 1920, as workers filled the jobs in the new steel mills. Like most cities in the Northeast and Midwest, Youngstown became a city of immigrants (Fuechtmann, 1989).

The year 1959 marked the date when the American steel industry changed. For the first time since the turn of the twentieth century, due to a 116-day industry-wide labor strike, the United States imported more steel than it exported (Fuechtmann, 1989). Following the steel strike of 1959 and into the 1970s, it was increasingly apparent to American manufacturers that a combination of the political-economic climate and technological advancement permitted foreign steel imports to be a more realistic alternative as the United States did not produce enough steel for its needs (Fuechtmann, 1989). With the collapse of American steel, manufacturing work declined drastically as a share of total number of jobs in Ohio since 1969 (Hill, 2001).

By late summer 1977 the steel industry in Youngstown suffered a final, deadly blow when 6,600 basic steel jobs were eliminated from the Mahoning Valley (Fuechtmann, 1989). The Youngstown Sheet and Tube Campbell Works officially closed on September 19, 1977. The shutdown was an economic disaster that represented a permanent loss both to individual workers and to the community as a whole (Fuechtmann, 1989). The shutdown caused an extended period of unemployment for blue-collar workers and a significant loss of tax revenue for local communities. The shutdown increased the burden on social services, as capital was drawn from the local community with no immediate prospect for replacement of the lost investment (Fuechtmann, 1989). Thousands of workers were unemployment overnight and the local economy suffered an immediate negative effect.

During the 1977 steel mill closings in the Mahoning Valley, there were no federal laws addressing worker notification of a shutdown. The Worker Adjustment and Retraining Notification Act (WARN) was enacted August 4, 1988 and became effective on February 4, 1989. The WARN Act required employers to notify workers at least

60 days in advance of a plant shutdown (DOLETA, n.d.). The immediate effects of the steel mill closings in the late 1970s left Youngstown economically wounded, as workers did not anticipate the shutdown or plan for its widespread ramifications.

The drastic decline in labor employment in Youngstown heavily contributed to the extreme double-dip recession that started in 1979 and ended in 1983 when average real incomes declined in Ohio (Hill, 2001). The transition from the Second Wave economy into the Third Wave economy has been particularly difficult for Youngstown and the communities of the Mahoning Valley. The steel and industrial manufacturing workforce abruptly suffered loss and the community struggled to recover, both economically and socially, through the decades that followed.

Youngstown Sheet and Tube

Second Wave Religious Attitudes and Deindustrialization

Understanding the religious attitudes that shaped the Second Wave help explain the economic and social changes that were brought about by the Second Wave. The religious underpinnings of Second Wave ideology explains in part the motivations that triggered industrialism and launched modern capitalism into a wealth generating sociopolitical economic machine. The religious attitudes of the Second Wave forever impacted the culture and economic attitudes of Youngstown.

The early sociologist Max Weber (1864-1920) defined the theologically infused economic principle known as "The Protestant Ethic" in *The Protestant Ethic and the Spirit of Capitalism* (1904). The spirit of capitalism was, according to Weber, an *ethos*, "... not mere business astuteness, but the idea of a duty of the individual toward the increase of his capital, which is assumed as an end in itself" (Weber, 1958). The Protestant Ethic engendered the idea that the harder one works and the more property and capital one accumulates, the godlier one becomes. Protestant Puritans saw property and capital as a divine calling of which they were stewards, liberals saw property as a self-evident natural right for private persons (Stackhouse, 1984). The concept of increased individual capital was foundational to the success of industrialism, mass production, and factory labor in the United States in the late nineteenth and early twentieth centuries.

According to Weber the success of capitalism depended on the embrace and internalization of certain socio-religious values. Weber noted that during the Industrial Revolution, it was not the capitalistic entrepreneurs of the commercial aristocracy who were the predominant bearers of the spirit of capitalism; it was, according to Weber, much more the rising strata of the lower industrial class (Weber, 1958). Weber argued that Protestants who did not come from dynastical families of Europe were empowered by the Protestant Ethic to commence the entrepreneurial industrialization of the

American manufacturing enterprise. The principle of vocation in the Protestant Ethic affirmed the necessary freedom for persons in society to perform pregiven patterns of social role and to give social space for the working out of godly duty. The logical and social psychology of the argument were vital to the development of cities in the Western World where "...peasants and freemen became artisans, tradesmen, merchants, and manufacturers, and above all citizens with self-governing responsibilities", leading to innovative social change (Stackhouse, 1984, p.59).

Blackburn (1997) argued that the Protestant Ethic was based on the self-righteous dogma that those who worked hard were rewarded by getting rich while those who were poor only had their own lack of hard work and thrift to blame (Blackburn, 1997). The harsh realities of the dogma of the Protestant Ethic were eventually manifest in the American labor crises following the Industrial Revolution. Weber did not ignore the fact that the earliest Lutheran formation of the Protestant ethic of capitalism was that the only way of living acceptably before God was solely through the fulfillment of the obligations imposed upon the individual by his position in the world. Fulfillment of worldly duties under all circumstances was the only way to live acceptably to God, according to the earlier Protestant Ethic, as individuals should abide by his living and let the godless run after gain (Weber, 1958). Prosperity, according to the earliest puritanical form of the Protestant ethic, was more concerned with the promotion of the divine calling that encouraged profit through hard work. Spending capital on personal luxuries was disrespectful to God; profits were expected to be poured back into individual callings.

Puritan values were eventually usurped, according to Weber, and replaced by a system of capitalism that no longer required ascetic values for its perpetuation. The shift occurred during the aggressive industrialization of the United States in the decades following the 1850s (Eckel, 1920). According to Stackhouse (1984), the first true test of American Human Rights philosophy was during the Civil War, where the issue was not only concerning the ethical veracity of slavery, but the conflict between burgeoning commercial and manufacturing economies of the north that was threatened by the southern plantation owners. The Civil War economy stimulated an American entry into the Industrial Revolution and corporations as social institutions became less a covenantal fellowship of those called to be responsible stewards for the glory of God and mutated into a legal fiction by which to gain wealth (Stackhouse, 1984). Weber believed that the new emphasis of the spirit of capitalism caused material goods to gain an unparalleled control over the individual which led to the more aggressive form of materialism that later concerned Karl Marx.

Due to the rise of a technical civilization, the Protestant ethic began to erode to a secularized, hollowed-out version of the work ethic, according to Colson and Eckerd (1991). Erosion was illustrated by Calvin Coolidge, who said, "He who builds a factory, builds a temple, and he who works there, worships there" (as reported by Colson and Eckard, 1991, p.39). Factory labor demanded workers who showed up on time, who would take orders from a management hierarchy without questioning, and were prepared to slave away at machines or in offices, performing brutally repetitive operations (Toffler, 1980). As work processes were deskilled and routinized, workers were subjected to intense scrutiny (Budd & Brimlow, 2002). The transformation of the Protestant ethic sparked a corresponding development of a social emphasis in religion that fell in the last decades of the nineteenth century (Mathews, 1927). As industrialization became part of the American experience, for both American Protestants and European Catholic immigrants, religious communities focused on urban-industrial problems (Fuechtmann, 1989). A strong emphasis on community, justice, and activism characterized the religious attitudes of the Second Wave and formulated religious response to industrialization and deindustrialization.

Second Wave Religious Attitudes: Community focused

The turn of the twentieth century brought with it the peak of American industrialism and increased factory labor as rumors of jobs invited disadvantaged immigrants from Europe (Stackhouse, 1984). America urbanized with pockets of ethnic communities scattered throughout the northeast. Immigrants settled in cities as American industrial workers. Primarily Catholic, the immigrants strived to provide a better standard of living for their families through the abundant work opportunities that were available in industrial America. Lance Morrow (1981) asserted that the immigrant work ethic came at last to merge with the Protestant work ethic. Kurth (1999) noted that, it was the religious faith and the religious community that supported immigrant workers.

Second Wave religious attitudes were marked by a communitarian worldview that stressed the horizontal aspect of religion: the call to demonstrate love toward one's neighbor by building community among interdependent individuals (Penning & Smidt, 2002). Independent labor organizations emerged during the American industrialism. The labor organizations, or unions, were found singing hymns on the picket lines, demonstrating that workers could form solidarities as independent congregations recapitulated in the economic sphere from earlier theological constructs of human rights (Stackhouse, 1984). In the face of deplorable working conditions, long hours, unsafe equipment, and low wages, laborers found a religious solidarity in mass organization.

At the turn of the nineteenth century, American Catholicism grew rapidly due to the inflow of European immigrant laborers. Catholics interpreted social concern as a missionary field open to conversion. The clergy of ethnic parishes had a multifunctional social role; the idea that clergy should be concerned about jobs and the social and economic welfare of people was a prevailing view (Fuechtmann, 1989). The new pastoral strategy of American Catholicism was adaptive rather than defensive (Feuchtmann, 1989). Because the majority of immigrant Catholic parishioners were laborers, the Catholic Church took a strong interest in organized labor. The openness of the Catholic Church to organized labor was formalized in 1891 by Leo XIII in his encyclical *Rerum Novarum*. An early alliance between the Catholic Church and American labor was a significant factor in preventing the emergence of a revolutionary labor movement in the United States (Abell, 1968). The Jesuits formed labor schools to train workers in union organization and industrial relations (Feuchtmann, 1989).

The American Catholic Church argued that work was not an individualistic enterprise; rather it was social (Russo & Corbin, 1999). Whereas American Catholicism was not as committed to capitalism as the proponents of the Protestant ethic, it viewed socialism as a poor alternative as "... bureaucracy, political tyranny, the helplessness of the individual as a factor of the ordering of his own life, and in general social inefficiency and decadence" (Catholic Bishops of the United States, no.33, 1919).

The American Bishops criticized the American Federation of Labor for its failure to demand or imply that the workers should never aspire to become owners as well as users of the instruments of production (Catholic Bishops of the United States: no.6, 1919). The Bishops recommended improving labor conditions, advocacy for a minimum legal wage, government housing for workers, and social insurance. In 1933 the bishops called for rigorous application of moral principles to big corporations and advocated for smaller units of business and production, admonishing that local communities should take pride in economic growth (Catholic Bishops of the United States: no.72, 1933). Post Vatican II American Catholicism demonstrated a slight shift from justice to charity and emphasized that the mission of the church was to achieve a conversion of heart, a growth in compassion, and sensitivity to the needs of brothers in want (Feuchtmann, 1989).

Second Wave Religious Attitudes: Justice-Oriented

According to Toffler (1980), the Second Wave brought with it a redefinition of God, justice, and love. A coherent worldview emerged that not only explained but justified Second Wave reality (Toffler, 1980). New theological ideas emerged as a response to the evils of industrialism, addressing its spiritual implications and social repercussions. The clergy of the Second Wave recognized that the ills of urban society were not simply the result of human depravity but reflected structural injustice (Penning & Smidt, 2002).

As the abuses of industrialism interminably increased, the response from the religious community was bold. Although some industrialists argued that the exploitation of labor was a necessary byproduct of industrialization, Gardner (1914) discounted the notion that some men oppressed and exploited others, which had no more moral significance than that wolves devoured lambs. Gardner argued that man was an intelligent and moral being with an increasing ability to control natural forces so that they worked out on the human level only beneficent results (Gardner, 1914). The ethical struggles of the Second Wave caused religious communities to rethink their role in society as industrialists exploited laborers. The call for justice energized the movements for labor organization and religious solidarity. Second Wave religion, in turn, envisioned redemption of society in the world (Penning & Smidt, 2002).

Cardinal Suenens (1983), a leader in the charismatic Catholic movement, described two polarities in the Christian community: the conservative churches whose tendency was to remain neutral in social matters and the progressive churches that sought to liberate human society through the gospel and therefore challenge every form of established disorder (Suenens & Camara, 1979). According to Suenens, justice must be respected and rendered to both God and mankind inseparably; poor and rich alike were entitled, in Christian justice, to be nourished by religion. The establishment of justice was the fundamental duty of man, but justice concerned both God and one's neighbor (Suenens & Camara, 1979).

Gardner (1914) argued that if an individual in society was superior, according to the ethic of Jesus, he should use that superiority of power in the interest of others. It was apparent that the injustices of actual society arose from the fact that men used power selfishly and that the strong used exceptional power primarily in personal interest. Social order, according to Gardner, could not be maintained without some element of the ethic of Jesus, as a measure of mutual services.

Gardner (1914) maintained that social peace and cooperation was secured only by the full acceptance of the paradoxical principle of Jesus that the strong shall serve the weak. Gardner asserted that the superiority of some individuals in society would not bar the way to self-realization of others, but would rather open to them the doors of higher possibilities; and the strongest cohesive force in society were the clasped hands of the strong and the weak. In a social configuration, Gardner believed that the value of each individual in society was capitalized as a value for all (Gardner, 1914). In like manner, Pope Leo XIII incorporated some tenants of socialist thought in his insistence that the state, or government, play an active role in the redistribution of wealth, property protection, and workers' rights in the name of justice and not just charity (as reported by Russo & Corbin, 1999).

Second Wave Religious Attitudes: Activism-oriented

At the end of the nineteenth century the transition from the dominance of Protestant ethic Puritanism to more socially oriented religious attitudes was a transition largely provoked by the impact of American industrialism (Johnson, 1973). Simultaneously, the rise of modern social science gave scholars new conceptual methods for understanding the social forces that affected the Church's mission (Fuechtmann, 1989). Within a generation the Industrial Revolution created such problems for religion as to lead to a vigorous enunciation of a social ethic by alert religious leaders (Handy, 1949). Religious communities were increasingly engaged in social issues. Second Wave religious attitudes of community and justice informed a call to social activism. Factions of the mainline Protestant denominations, both puritanical and liberal, saw the need for a fundamental public theology to give affirmative shape to social institutions and to combat the superpersonal forces of evil in society. Walter Rauschenbusch (1861-1918) and other theologians in mainline Christianity introduced and promoted the social gospel as an alternative to the prevailing forms of the Protestant Ethic (Stackhouse, 1984).

The Social Gospel affirmed the concept of the Church conquering social evils, superpersonal forces according to Rauschenbusch, to eventually Christianize all of society through social activism. The attempt of the Social Gospel illustrated the rediscovery in Protestant theology of the social dimension of the Church's mission as a voice for social justice (Fuechtmann, 1989). Realistic laymen were largely untouched by the social gospel and did not share the official social passion of the communion to which they belonged. That the social gospel was not popularized at the lay level was probably the fault of the clergy (Meyer, 1970). Even though liberal clergy clung to the ideals of the social gospel, it had little impact on a grass roots level.

By the 1920s, the social gospel had run its course, but it took the stock market crash of 1929 to destroy the illusion of Social Christianity (King, 1981). Handy (1960) noted that the period between World Wars I and II was a period of "… religious destitution not less severe than that of the concomitant moral and economic depression" (p.3). Karl Barth (1886-1968) saw in the German experience the danger of canonizing political arrangements as a Christian society (Fuechtmann, 1989). Proponents of the social gospel gleaned credit for the New Deal social programs and the success of the West in the World Wars.

Reinhold Niebuhr (1892-1971) criticized the failures of the social gospel, recognizing that its premise was unrealistic. Niebuhr did not find activism an unrealistic method to achieve justice. Serving as pastor of a church in Detroit, Michigan, Niebuhr was an outspoken critic of Henry Ford. Troubled by the demoralizing effects of industrialism on the workers, Niebuhr allowed union organizers to use his pulpit to expound their message of workers' rights. Niebuhr documented inhumane conditions created by the assembly lines and erratic employment practices. Niebuhr advocated a Christian realism, as opposed to the idealism of the social gospel, preaching that in social crises the best that could be hoped for was justice. Niebuhr (1920) noted following the First World War:

> *The church knows what is occupying the mind of the world and it is anxious to satisfy that interest. If it expresses liberal or radical sentiments on current industrial or social problems it frequently betrays a greater desire to "hold the workingman for the church" than to establish justice for him (p.588).*

Niebuhr's criticism of the social gospel and his program for theological and political renewal helped churches recover from the period of Protestant downturn between the World Wars (Johnson, 1982). The work of Niebuhr contributed to the later social activism of mainline Protestantism in the early second half of the twentieth century.

The Prominence of Mainline Protestantism and Roman Catholicism at the End of the Second Wave

As the Second Wave drew to a close, liberal Protestant clergy remained socially active in the political controversies of the 1960s (Quinley, 1974). After the Civil Rights movement, American Protestant clergy learned something about political protest and were willing to make general connections between religion and public policy (Fuechtmann, 1989). Mainline Protestants and Roman Catholics were once socially active in battling the ill-effects of industrialization, but by the 1970s they found themselves battling the ill-effects of deindustrialization. The labor crises of the 1970s elicited a new response from Protestant clergy toward American manufacturing and labor relations as America transitioned into the Third Wave society and economy.

The 1976 General Conference of the United Methodist Church issued a positional paper entitled, *Unemployment: 1976 General Conference Statement* stating that every citizen of the United States had a right to meaningful, useful, rewarding employment contributing to the public good at a wage that was supportive of an adequate standard of living with human dignity. The 188th General Assembly of the Presbyterian Church released a 1976 study exploring neighborhood-based models for job creation. The 11th General Synod of the United Church of Christ called for a reaffirmation to the God-given right of all persons to useful and remunerative work, together with the responsibility to provide for themselves and their dependents. As the unemployment rate increased in urban areas of the Northeast and Midwest, in 1975 the Catholic bishops declared that opportunities for work should be provided for all able and willing to work (Catholic Bishops of the United States, 1975).

The Ecumenical Coalition of the Mahoning Valley

Second Wave religious attitudes toward industrialization and deindustrialization culminated in the 1977 steel crises of Youngstown. Fuechtmann (1989) published *Steeples and Stacks* documenting the involvement of religious communities in the 1977 crisis of closing steel mills. The text documented the tragic story of the failed effort by clergy and steelworkers to save the Youngstown Sheet and Tube's Campbell Works in hopes that the telling of the story would help future efforts on behalf of working people and their communities to succeed (Fuechtmann, 1989). Fuechtmann noted that the Youngstown steel mill closings were an example of the kind of "... deindustrialization that requires blind faith in the economic theory to see the sun behind very obvious gray clouds" (Fuechtmann 1989, p.3).

Feuchtmann's *Steeples and Stacks*

Fuechtmann maintained that the community response to the Youngstown steel crisis was seen as a new development in the interaction of religion and public affairs in American life. Youngstown was seen as the testing ground for a different model of local community action in the face of deindustrialization and economic crisis (Fuechtmann, 1989). Even though the Ecumenical Coalition did not succeed in saving the steel industry in Youngstown, the efforts of the coalition provided a basis for people in other local communities to better understand economic struggles (Fuechtmann, 1989).

Fuechtmann (1989) noted that although communities suffering economic loss from a natural disaster depended on the Army National Guard, the Red Cross, and countless volunteer agencies, the city of Youngstown had no hope for the disaster it faced with the closing of its primary steel mill. The religious Ecumenical Coalition formed as an emergency response agency to serve the local community where traditional institutions failed (Fuechtmann, 1989). Second Wave religious attitudes fueled the response of the religious community in Youngstown to organize the coalition and respond to the economic crisis that the city of Youngstown faced.

Episcopal bishop Charles Rawlings saw the problems of American cities as rooted in the foundations of economic and social arrangements and the Youngstown crisis of 1977 as an opportunity for the churches to deal with the urban-industrial crisis at a fundamental and revolutionary level (Fuechtmann, 1989). With Roman Catholic bishop James Malone, head of the Catholic diocese in Youngstown, Rawlings organized a meeting with several clergy from different denominations to discuss what effects the shutdown would have on the lives of the people in the church pews and what kind of pastoral response was called for from the religious community (Fuechtmann, 1989). Following the meeting, it was apparent that the clergy leaders were committed to action and not just talk (Fuechtmann, 1989). The Ecumenical Coalition was formed and a Steel Crisis Conference was held at the Youngstown First Presbyterian Church in October of 1977 (Fuechtmann, 1989). Until then, religious leaders had kept their distance from Youngstown party politics (Fuechtmann, 1989). The internal dynamic of the religious sector in Youngstown was characterized by an inclination to take action in the sociopolitical sphere and adopt a cooperative interfaith strategy (Fuechtmann, 1989).

The Ecumenical Coalition arrived at the conclusion that local community ownership of abandoned industries might be a solution to the economic crisis. Work rapidly proceeded to allocate the estimated $535 million required to achieve the objective of reopening the closed facilities and resuming steel production. The Coalition believed that efforts to restore steel production would ultimately be assisted by Washington as part of an overall program of steel revitalization (Fuechtmann, 1989). The United States Department of Housing and Urban Development responded by stating that the commendable community support was precisely the sort of local effort they were looking for in developing new Federal strategies to support areas like Youngstown that were determined to help themselves when faced with devastating plant closings. The congressman of Youngstown's district remarked that the plan was ill-conceived and ill-advised (as reported by Fuechtmann, 1989).

A pastoral letter issued by the Ecumenical Coalition in November 1977 described the theological basis for the response of the coalition and highlighted the Second Wave religious attitudes of community, justice, and activism. The letter included the following declarations: (a) human beings and community life were higher values than corporate profits, (b) economic life took place in a moral context, (c) Jesus identified himself with the poor and victims of injustice, (d) economic decisions ought not to be left to the judgment of a few persons with economic power, and (e) power should be shared with the larger community that was affected by the decisions (as reported by Fuechtmann, 1989). The letter was largely well received by the community and rallied a public response.

The Coalition achieved federal government financing via the Department Housing and Urban Development and soon transformed from an emergent crisis response group into an organization with a $750,000 budget developing a project involving $500,000,000 (Fuechtmann, 1989). The goals of the Coalition were broadened to include political action on a national scale. In order to ensure an equal voice of religious representation, the Coalition repeatedly added new personnel from varying denominations and religious groups rather than adding functional expertise. Few members of the Coalition had knowledge of steelmaking; the Coalition was almost totally dependent on outside consultants. The decision-making structure of the Coalition included no one with expertise in steel management or corporate finance and the Coalition did not have within its ranks anyone capable of evaluating the work of consultants. Tension increased between the frustrated business community and the clergy-operated Coalition, support from the steelworkers unions was perpetually frustrated, and the unemployed steelworkers lent little volunteer support to the cause (Fuechtmann, 1989).

As realistic operational expenses and projected profits were assembled in a plan for operating the steel mill, it was increasingly clear that the Coalition was ill-equipped to proceed with the project. Proposals sent to Washington to secure funding from the Carter administration were either stalled or rejected. The United States Economic Development Administration identified substantive weaknesses in the final proposal for funding submitted by the Coalition (Fuechtmann, 1989). After other failed efforts in Washington, the participating Presbyterians withdrew from the Coalition with others following suit arguing that to continue to struggle would be inconsistent with the realities of the situation and would leave the Coalition open to the charge of engendering false hopes. Lacking both funds and time to continue work or to develop another proposal for funding, the Coalition closed its offices on June 1, 1979. The corporate structure of the organization remained in place as religious leaders did not wish to give steelworkers the impression that they were abandoning their concern for the unemployed. The attempt of the Coalition to save the Youngstown Sheet and Tube Campbell Works was unsuccessful. Had the Coalition restored laborers to work without raising further moral questions for future generations, the Coalition would have been an even greater failure (Fuechtmann, 1989).

Even though the Ecumenical Coalition in Youngstown did not achieve its intended goals, the Coalition was ahead of its time as pioneers in uncharted territory. The Coalition helped a community in the northeastern rustbelt learn that an economic future cannot be taken for granted and local communities such as Youngstown cannot afford to be passive. The coalition wrote a valuable chapter from which future efforts in religion and public affairs learn (Fuechtmann, 1989). The task of evaluating ethical economic questions in the religious sector was far heavier and lasted much longer than the religious leaders of the Coalition imagined. The failure of the Ecumenical Coalition highlighted the beginning of the end of the Second Wave in Youngstown and stood as a symbol for all rust-belt cities of the reality and hardships of the transitions to the Third Wave.

CHAPTER 3
Third Wave Economics in Youngstown

The Third Wave of Demassified Technology

Weber (tr. 1958) recognized that the modern Western form of capitalism was strongly influenced by the development of technological possibilities. Unlike previous waves of progress, the Third Wave was peculiarly characterized by technology. Toffler (1994) noted an early indication of a technological shift in society and industry when the Second Wave's smokestack economy was fading and a new Third Wave economy was born. The indication of the approaching end of the Second Wave was in 1956, the first year in which white-collar and service employees outnumbered blue-collar factory workers in the United States (Toffler, 1994). The Third Wave followed with a rapid increase of technology, including the emergence of cellular telephones, satellite television, and the Internet, outmoding the older forms of Second Wave industrialism. Populations that once relied on mass media and social structures were individually empowered by personal computers and consumer credit in the Third Wave.

At the helm of the Third Wave organized labor, pounded by years of union-busting and deindustrialization, decreased to less than 10% of the private-sector workforce and seemed to disappear altogether from the popular consciousness (Frank, 2000). Service jobs replaced many of the well-paid positions lost in manufacturing. In the Third Wave American jobs created by high-tech globalization replaced the low-tech jobs lost to competition under Free Trade agreements (Cetron & Davies, 2005). There was no direct demand for labor in the Third Wave economy. Instead, demand for labor was derived from product demand, the goods and services workers made, which sparked demand for people to make them (Hill, 2001). Organized labor, once dominant in the Second Wave, was eclipsed by the demands of an individualistic Third Wave workforce driven by technological advancement.

The old paradigm of unions versus corporations was obsolete in the Third Wave (Cetron & Davies, 2005). Member unions withdrew from the American Federation of Labor - Congress of Industrial Organizations (AFL-CIO) because of disputes over the politicization of the labor movement (Youngstown Vindicator, September 4, 2006). In place of unions and corporations negotiating for mutual benefit, the Third Wave brought powerful forces inspiring demands for greater transparency and accountability in large institutions; a product of the demands by Second Wave religious demands for social justice in deindustrialization (Cetron & Davies, 2005). Greater transparency and greater corporate responsibility to care for workers affected by downsizing in the transition from the Second Wave set the Third Wave manufacturing crises apart from the labor crises of the Second Wave. Where corporations were more open to scrutiny and organized labor was a less relevant factor, the Third Wave was symbolized by a demassification of industry, society, and economics.

As society increasingly demassified, according to Toffler (1980), the media, families, and even religion followed suit (Toffler, 1980). In the Third Wave, the market and the people were both understood as grand principles of social life rather than particulars and were seen as one in the same (Frank, 2000). Kurth (1999) identified a new individualistic ideology characterized by consumer sovereignty in economics that dominated the Third Wave. The amount of outstanding consumer credit more than doubled between 1980 and 1990 (Philips, 2006). Consumerism and individualism reigned supreme in the Third Wave society and economy.

An increase in individualism was one of the major social changes that occurred in the West during the second half of the twentieth century (Crompton, 2002). Beginning in the 1970s, American political and intellectual elites began to promote the ideology of universal human rights as the rights of individuals (Kurth, 1999). The more contemporary concept of individual human rights stood in contrast with earlier social movements where the rights of entire social segments such as labor union and racial groups were emphasized over individual rights (Collins, 2005). Second Wave religion lobbied for the rights of women, laborers, and African Americans. Human rights philosophy in the Third Wave, particularly in Third Wave economies, emphasized individual human rights over the rights of groups.

Toffler (1980) urged that there would be a clash of civilizations between social segments committed to maintaining the Second Wave and social segments committed to Third Wave progress. Toffler predicted that society would be divided between Second Wave people committed to maintaining the dying order and Third Wave people committed to constructing a radically different tomorrow (Toffler 1980). Deindustrialized cities like Youngstown illustrated Toffler's predictions, as 2007 manufacturing crises provoked conflict between Second Wave and Third Wave social divisions. Individualistic consumers of the Third Wave clashed with the community-oriented labor force of the Second Wave.

Although Toffler and other futurists predicted the economic shift from industrial manufacturing to information technology for some time, American labor unions did not collectively heed the call. In Youngstown and similar cities across the rust belt of America, Second Wave political lobbies and labor unions continued to cling to the power of the unskilled American labor of Second Wave industrialism (Toffler, 2004). The transition into the Third Wave was stifled by Second Wave resistance to Third Wave economic and social trends.

Third Wave Industry and Youngstown Manufacturing

Youngstown State University director of the Center for Working Class Studies Dr. John Russo (2004) noted that the consolidation of corporate capitalism, a reality of the Third Wave, produced "… a decades-long cultural war of titanic proportions, played on local battlefields across the United States" (Russo 2004, p.628). Youngstown was a local battlefield upon which a battle to transition into the Third Wave was fought. Since the 1990s, the Youngstown metropolitan area was the laggard in per capita income growth among the cities of Ohio. Since the per capita income plummeted from 1979 to the mid-1980s, the Youngstown area recovered slowly compared to the rest of the state of Ohio. Hill (2006) noted that even if a corporation was multinational, it directly affected local communities in which it operated: if the product died, the town suffered (Hill, 2001). The downsizing of labor from large corporations induced economic suffering upon Youngstown. The effects of deindustrialization, both in 1977 and in 2007, were evident in the Mahoning Valley.

Safford (2004) compared the transition from deindustrialization of Youngstown and a similar Pennsylvania rustbelt city, Allentown. Safford found that a variety of factors contributed to Youngstown being trapped in the Second Wave framework, whereas Allentown prospered into a high-tech Third Wave economy. Safford (2004) noted that:

> *Allentown can be characterized as having adhered to the high-road which has involved the transformation of existing companies to make them competitive on a global scale, attracting inward investment of high-skill jobs and the emergence of a strong entrepreneurial sector. Youngstown, on the other hand, has suffered from an inability to develop a coherent approach to attracting inward investment, a lack of entrepreneurship, and the*

inability of major local employers to transform in ways that benefit the community (p.27).

Hill (2001) identified a strong positive relationship between the size of a metropolitan area, job generation, and growth in per capita income among the labor market areas of Ohio. Even though the state of Ohio was predominantly transitioning out of manufacturing labor and into high-tech industry, the anomaly was the Youngstown metropolitan area, the major reason for the relatively weak income performance of the state as a whole (Hill, 2001). Youngstown demonstrated an economic and social resistance to the Third Wave.

Deindustrialization in Youngstown began with the shift from steel labor to manufacturing labor in the Mahoning Valley in the early 1970s. The transition of labor employment out of the city of Youngstown to the neighboring Trumbull County began with the growth of the Packard Electric (now Delphi Corporation) and General Motors Lordstown plants in the 1970s; with the shift came significant population decline in the city of Youngstown (Fuechtmann, 1989). The trend of population decline continued a steady -3.4% population decline in the 2003 U.S. Census. The shift brought suburbanization with the rising affluence of laborers (Fuechtmann 1989, p.23).

Between 1970 and 1980, in the decade of the 1977 steel mill crisis, the Mahoning Valley area collectively experienced a 6.8% increase in employment. During the same period, the city of Youngstown experienced a -21.6% decline in employment, an apparent affect of the Youngstown Sheet and Tube Campbell Works closing at the end of the decade. The greater Youngstown area experienced a steady decline in manufacturing employment after 1996, when manufacturing labor comprised under 60,000 area jobs, compared to 40,000 in 2006 U.S. Bureau of Labor Statistics report. As the suburban communities of the Mahoning Valley slowly recovered, the urban city of Youngstown continued to experience economic decline.

The suburbanization of labor and industry and the shifting population trends set the 2007 manufacturing crises apart from the steel crises of the 1970s. In the decade between 1980 and 1990, the Mahoning Valley area experienced a collective decline in employment of -2.1% and the city of Youngstown experienced a decline of employment of -23.1%. In the subsequent decade of 1990 to 2000, the Mahoning Valley experienced an increase of employment by 4.5% and employment in the city of Youngstown declined at -5.0%; a nevertheless significant improvement from the decade prior, demonstrating some economic recovery. Spanning three decades from 1970 to 2000, the Mahoning Valley experienced a 9.2% increase in employment while the city of Youngstown experienced a -42.8% decline according to the 2000 US Census. The increase in employment in the suburban areas of the Mahoning Valley, compared to the decrease in employment in the city of Youngstown, demonstrated the suburbanization of work that was characteristic of the Third Wave society and economy. The urbanization of life and work was characteristic of the Second Wave society, but the suburbanization of life and work was characteristic of the Third Wave society. The suburbanization of the Third Wave made the issues surrounding current labor crises distinct from earlier labor struggles.

Another significant difference between the 1977 steel crisis and the manufacturing crises of 2007 is the manner in which employers downsized the labor force. Whereas in 1977 job-elimination was abrupt and employees were left with little benefits or time to prepare, the Mahoning Valley employers offered lump sum buyouts to employees, providing a period for preparation and negotiation with the unions. In the summer of 2006 General Motors announced that it would eliminate the third shift of autoworkers from the Lordstown, Ohio facility, the largest employer in the Mahoning Valley, because the plant was so efficient that it was still producing more cars than the market will bear. The downsizing of General Motors would inevitably result in an overall decrease in GM's $675 million payroll in the Mahoning Valley. In 2006, Ford Motor Company said it wanted to trim 30,000 positions from its payroll over the next several years; [General Motors] wants to cut a similar number" (McDougal, 2006). The United Autoworkers Union Local 112 of the Mahoning Valley reported that at the Lordstown assembly plant, 1,090 of the 3,800 hourly workers registered for employee buyouts offered by the company in lieu of direct job elimination (Youngstown Vindicator, June 27, 2006). Following a 41-hour labor national labor strike in September 2007, the United Autoworkers reached a tentative agreement with General Motors; the strike was the first of its kind in 30 years.

Delphi Automotive, parts supplier for General Motors and the Mahoning Valley's second largest employer, offered aged employees a buyout incentive to eliminate surplus jobs in a corporate restructuring plan during bankruptcy. The buyouts were part of an effort to provide early retirement incentives to Delphi workers as the Troy, Michigan-based company sought to streamline its work force. Approximately 7,500 hourly workers represented by the International Union of Electronic Workers and Communications Workers of America were eligible to participate, and 84% agreed to leave the company. As a result of the buyout, some IUE represented employees were offered a lump sum payment of $35,000 to retire while eligible employees could decide to accept buyout packages ranging from $40,000 to $140,000. Employees accepting buyouts gave up all benefits except for vested, accrued pensions (Youngstown Vindicator August 19, 2006). Delphi told union officials that it wanted to slash hourly wages from $27 to $10, cut benefits, close plants and eliminate jobs (Youngstown Vindicator, November 4, 2006). On a national scale, 47,600 hourly workers decided to leave General Motors and Delphi Corporation through buyout or early retirement offers (Youngstown Vindicator, June 27, 2006). In the summer of 2007, Delphi employees agreed to significant wage reductions.

Some Youngstown area manufacturers were not aligned with the more ethical approaches to Third Wave downsizing demonstrated by other corporations. The peripheral Mahoning Valley employer and the nation's largest ladder manufacturer, Werner Company, located just across the Pennsylvania state border, filed for Chapter 11 bankruptcy in June 2006. The bankruptcy filing was, according to company officials, part of a corporate strategy of moving ladder production to Mexico and China (Youngstown Vindicator, June 14, 2006).

In 2003 Werner Company shut down its ladder-making operations in Greenville, eliminating 500 jobs. The company shut down other plants in the United States the next year and moved more production overseas. According to Werner Company officials, the moves were forced by major retail customers who wanted less-expensive ladders from other countries" (Youngstown Vindicator, June 14, 2006). Pennsylvania lost 123,800 manufacturing jobs between January 2001 and January 2006, a 16% higher loss on both the state and national levels according to the Steel Valley Authority.

Jim Paynard, president of the Pennsylvania Manufacturer's Association, stated that "… the job losses are gutting the American middle class" and that steelworkers were the victims of economic terrorism (Youngstown Vindicator, November 11, 2003). According to the labor-union website "Stand Up for Steel", there were 39 steel companies in bankruptcy in the United States (http://www.standupforsteel.org). Whereas labor union leaders identified bankruptcy of steel companies and manufacturers as a result of unfair trade practices, the Toffler model identified the crisis as an industry-wide failure to adapt to Third Wave principles. The Third Wave adaptation failure model blamed both labor and management across the manufacturing industries.

National Trends and Manufacturing Labor Decline

The trends of labor and unemployment in the United States and Ohio were consistent with Toffler's predictions for the Third Wave. In America, less than one worker in six was employed in manufacturing and according to 2007 trends, manufacturing would potentially account for only one in ten American jobs by 2020. As the economy of a nation strengthens, it was inevitable that a smaller proportion of workers were needed by manufacturing, according to Rowthorn and Ramaswamy (1997). Employment in the manufacturing industry in wealthy economies fell from 28% in 1970 to 18% in 1994 (Rowthorn & Ramaswamy, 1997). In 2006 the United States Bureau of Labor Statistics reported that in the economy as a whole, manufacturing represented about 11% of all employment, yet less than 5% of all establishments (U.S. Bureau of Labor Statistics, NAICS 31-33).

Employment data demonstrated a consistent pattern with Third Wave predictions. The unemployment rate in the United States during the steel crisis of 1977 was 7.05%, two-thirds greater than the 4.7% unemployment rate as of August 2006. The unemployment rate in the greater Youngstown area was reported at 6.7% in July 2006 by the United States Bureau of Labor Statistics; a relatively low rate compared to the fluctuations between peaks of 10 and 11% in the 1990s according to the U.S. Bureau of Labor Statistics. Data from the Mass Layoff Statistics program showed that in 2005 there were 1,292 extended mass layoff events in manufacturing, resulting in 223,058 separations of workers from their jobs and 242,113 initial claimants for unemployment insurance across the United States.

Although manufacturing was not likely to experience growth in employment, there were some job opportunities because of substantial replacement needs in skilled production occupations (Ewald, 2004). Unemployment could fall if the rate of growth of actual output was faster than the rate of growth of potential output, which was given by the growth of productivity and the labor force (Robinson, 1988). The trends of unemployment concurred with the Tofflerian wave model, as productivity and profits increased in manufacturing while employment decreased in the Third Wave.

In 2005 the unemployment rate of persons most recently employed in manufacturing industries was 4.9%, according to the Current Population Survey of the United States Bureau of Labor Statistics. The overall unemployment rate was 5.1%. The 2005 layoff statistics were the lowest in the 1996-2005 periods (U.S. Bureau of Labor Statistics NAICS 31-33). The high rate of unemployment in the manufacturing industry was consistent with Third Wave predictions as laborers once employed by unskilled jobs searched for new opportunities for work. The more recent and lower layoff statistics demonstrated that the Second Wave was coming to a close as the Third Wave economy took root.

The United States Labor Department reported that in 2005 real hourly wages were 1.9% higher than in 2000, compared to the 1.1% rise in wages between 1990 and 1995 (Youngstown Vindicator, September 4, 2006). As layoff numbers decreased, unemployment numbers level and wages increased, the pain felt by the transition of the Second Wave economy was replaced by the alternatives of the Third Wave economy. Manufacturing and unskilled labor was the chief industry of the Second Wave; its significance was drastically minimized in the Third Wave.

The transition out of the Second Wave was often perceived as evidence of economic decline; on the contrary, it was a natural consequence of economic progress. According to the 1990 report by William Brock, Secretary of Labor under President Reagan, either the top third of the population would grow wealthier while the bottom two-thirds became progressively poorer, or America would slide into relative poverty together as exports and labor productivity decreased (as reported by Colson and Eckard 1991). The predictions of Brock were inaccurate, as manufacturing and labor productivity significantly increased due to the rapid technological advances of the Third Wave. While the American steel industry lost 350,000 jobs in the 1980s and 1990s, it was simultaneously technologically advanced and more productive (Youngstown Vindicator, November 11, 2003). Manufacturing productivity was $7,634 higher per worker in 1998 than it was in 1979 and nonmanufacturing productivity was $461 per worker lower (Hill, 2001). Productivity decreased in the Third Wave service sectors and increased in the Second Wave industrial sectors.

National Trends and Globalization

The technological shift in productivity that caused America to transition from an agricultural economy in the First Wave to an industrial economy in the Second Wave repeated as America transitioned from an industrial economy to an information economy in the Third Wave. Developing economies transitioned from the First Wave to the Second Wave as manufacturing was outsourced from the developed world and free trade and globalization was the standard practice in Third Wave economies. Supporters of Free Trade and outsourcing maintained that outsourcing was part of globalization and the evolution of the international marketplace (Dobbs, 2004).

Critics of the free trade and globalization that marked the Third Wave argued that policies leading to the transition to the Third Wave in America were characterized by "…knee-jerk, band-aid reactions rather than long-term planning" (Hira & Hira, 2005, p.7). Other opponents argued that the corporations of the Third Wave were characterized by a short-term mentality by cutting the lifeline that kept America strong and robust (Hira & Hira, 2005). Supporters of free trade saw competition as a byproduct of free market capitalism as countries and corporations adjusted to the introduction of new products and processes of production, made possible through technological innovation (Piderit, 1998)

Media commentator Lou Dobbs launched an aggressive campaign against American outsourcing. Dobbs (2004) maintained that corporate greed was the root cause of outsourcing labor and problems such as the increasing trade deficit and the creation of jobs sufficient to keep up with population growth crippled the United States economy. Dobbs stated that Americans were not losing their jobs to a dynamic, rapidly changing economy but to multinational corporations that forced American workers to compete with cheap foreign labor (Dobbs, 2004).

The Stand Up for Steel organization lobbied against both the Clinton and Bush administrations in the 1990s and 2000s in an attempt to pass a moratorium on Free Trade Laws to stop the import of foreign steel (Stand Up for Steel, 2006). Ohio Democratic congressman Denis Kusinich stated that the United States should withdraw from the World Trade Organization and require all trading partners to meet specific human rights and labor standards (as reported by Dobbs, 2004). Bruce Josten, executive vice president of the United States Chamber of Commerce, replied that he preferred outsourcing reform over a moratorium against free trade legislation. Josten suggested that politicians attempting to introduce legislation on the state-level to stop outsourcing should be halted (as reported by Dobbs, 2004). Concerning the often difficult transition to Third Wave economics, Weidenbaum (2004) warned that the United States should not initiate new national policy to respond to what were short-term developments. The transitional period between the Second and Third Wave was temporary.

Toffler (1994) recognized that behind the rhetoric of opponents of the Third Wave was the notion that the shift of employment from manual work to service and technological jobs was somehow bad for the economy and that a small manufacturing sector left the economy hollowed out (Toffler, 1994). Toffler maintained that the arrogance of the powerful smokestack companies of the Second Wave were to blame for the unnecessarily rocky transition into the Third Wave, and those who were least responsible for industrial backwardness and least able to protect themselves, their workers, were punished (Toffler, 1994). According to Toffler, the groups that were fighting to maintain the Second Wave were the groups that did the most harm to individual workers.

Toffler (1995) argued that Second Wave elites fought to retain or reinstate an unsustainable past because they gained wealth and power from applying Second Wave principles while middle-class and poor Americans also resisted the transition to the Third Wave out of fear that they would be left behind, lose their jobs, and slide further down the economic and social slope (Toffler, 1995). Such fears were confirmed by a report from the McKinsey Global Institute that found that at least 31% of workers regain employment after a layoff and many of those who were reemployed experienced substantial wage loss (Hira & Hira, 2005). The final stages of transition from a Second Wave economy to a Third Wave economy was not without casualties. According to Saks (1985) a healthy economy was constantly undergoing adjustments that were costly to some people and beneficial to others.

The Third Wave and Downsized Ohio Labor

Deindustrialization had macroimplications only in economies unable to absorb the workers released by manufacturing (Rowthorn & Ramaswamy, 1997). In Ohio attention was placed on the potential impact of labor supply as the workers of the baby-boomer generation began to retire (Ewald, 2004). Although in 2012 nearly two-thirds of the oldest baby-boomers in the 55-64 age range were expected to be working, there was more than 800,000 baby-boomers, 48-66 years old in 2012, leaving the labor force (Ewald, 2004). By 2010 the average retirement age in the United States was expected to be delayed well into the seventies (Cetron & Davies, 2005). The transition out of the Second Wave affected the aged workforce most significantly, as Third Wave trends such as mass layoffs, downsizing, and outsourcing transformed American manufacturing. Aged workers were most susceptible to the negative effects of the Third Wave transition as they were least likely to possess marketable technological skill or advanced education.

Third Wave workers were overworked, alienated, insecure, cynical and anxious about the future (Budd & Brimlow, 2002). A clear understanding of the skills demanded by Ohio's Third Wave technology industries needed development: an understanding that went beyond the entry level skill requirements for production operations that was characteristic of the Second Wave (Hill, 2001). Toffler (1994) noted that whereas low-skilled, essentially interchangeable muscle drove the Second Wave and mass factory-style education prepared workers for routine, repetitive labor, by contrast the Third Wave was accompanied by a growing noninterchangeability of labor as skill requirements skyrocketed. Toffler predicted that rising specialization and rapid changes in skill requirements reduced the interchangeability of labor (Toffler, 2004). The productive workforce of the Third Wave was required to be hard-working, literate, and numerate (Hill, 2001). In the Third Wave successful people were complex and individualistic. Education was interspersed and interwoven with work, and was more spread out over a lifetime (Toffler, 1980).

Vocational identity or occupational self-concept was a unique Third Wave experience of the individual worker's subjective perception of career goals, interests, and abilities; a concept that stood in contrast of the communal identity of organized labor in the Second Wave (Ebberwein, 2000). Calsouphes (1998) indicated that transitional midcareer workers reflected a rethinking of the meaning of work and its relationship to self-identity that exemplified an ongoing experience of internal transition about career that was distinct from specific external changes (Calsouphes, 1998).

To sustain the economic base of the state, Ohio's manufacturing leadership needed to form a strong forward-looking partnership with higher education to reinforce and advance the state's existing industry-driven technology base (Hill, 2001). Youngstown State University began the Center for Working Class Studies in 1996 under the direction of Dr. John Russo. Instead of investing funds and energy in an academic journal, the university initiated an education program with Local 1375 of the United Steel Workers of America, focused on retraining and vocational transition (Russo 1999).

In the Youngstown area a three-county team of employment counselors began contacting workers at five companies that announced layoffs throughout the Mahoning Valley. The counselors were supplied by Department of Job and Family Services. Counselors found that manufacturing employees were not ready to discuss their work life and some workers were in a state of denial over whether they needed retraining (Youngstown Vindicator, June 8, 2006). The manufacturing crises of 2007 were softened by addressing misconceptions regarding retraining and the demands of the Third Wave economy and society.

According to the Youngstown Warren Regional Chamber of Commerce, between 1970 and 1990, the percentage of area residents age 25 or higher with some college experience increased by 158% compared to 76% nationally, while the percentage with four or more years of college increased by 85% (Youngstown Area Regional Chamber of Commerce, 2006). Television station WYTV

Channel 33, an ABC affiliate, sponsored a "Steel to Scholars" program promoting high school graduation and post-secondary education in the Mahoning Valley and greater Youngstown area.

Programs such as the Center for Working Class Studies at Youngstown State University, employment counseling, and the Steel to Scholars program contributed to a less tragic transition into the Third Wave for Youngstown. As educational institutions, government officials, and community and religious leaders gave more attention to retraining the labor force, the economic fallout was less tragic for Youngstown as it moved out of the Second Wave.

CHAPTER 4
Third Wave Religious Attitudes in Youngstown

Third Wave Religious Attitudes and Deindustrialization

Mainline Protestant denominations were well represented among Roman Catholics in the Ecumenical Coalition of the Mahoning Valley during the 1977 Youngstown steel crisis, but the Evangelical and fundamentalist congregations were unaffiliated (Feuchtman, 1989). A shift in American religious life occurred that was consistent with the socioeconomic changes brought about by the advent of the Third Wave. Mainline Protestantism and Roman Catholicism were prominent in the Second Wave society and labor crises, but evangelicalism became prominent in American public life and the 2007 Third Wave manufacturing crises.

Early in the twentieth century Protestantism split into two factions: the liberal wing which remained dominant by accommodating theologically to forces of modernity, and a conservative wing that seemed, by the

1920s, to have submerged from public life (Hammond, 1985). Whereas Mainline Protestants and Roman Catholics focused on issues of social justice in the Second Wave, evangelicals withdrew their energies from political life and focused attention on evangelism (Penning & Smidt, 2002). The dominant religion of the Second Wave, mainline Protestants and Roman Catholics, gave way to evangelicalism as America transitioned into the Third Wave. Noll (2002) observed that the previously marginal evangelicals became larger and more prominent, but the previously central mainline denominations moved to the margins.

The American religious landscape changed with the American labor markets. The decline of manufacturing and labor in the Third Wave was consistent with a decline in Second Wave religion. Since 1965, liberal denominations declined at an average five-year rate of 4.6%, while evangelical denominations increased at an average five-year rate of 8% (Collins, 2005). Mainline Protestant denominations began to decline in America in the 1960s; mainly because clergy were often seen as too liberal for their congregations, siding with causes such as war-protests and civil rights (Philips, 2006).

According to Green (2004), evangelicals outnumbered mainline Protestants in the United States, comprising 26.3% of the population, compared to 16.0% for mainline Protestant. Roman Catholics comprised 17.5% of the population. In Third Wave America Muslims outnumbered Presbyterians and Episcopalians (Kimball, 2002). The mainline Denominations lost parishioners just as the industrial cities have bled jobs (Straub, 2006). Fundamentalist, right-wing churches grew rapidly.

Second Wave religion was downsized with Second Wave industry.

Second Wave religion remained significantly quiet during the 2007 manufacturing crises of Youngstown. Regnerus and Smith (1998) suggested that Mainline Protestants were more reserved since the activism of the social gospel movement early in the first half of the twentieth century and the Civil Rights movement in the second half of the twentieth century. Mainline Protestant churches were more privatized in their religious function and less concerned with public engagement. Regnerus and Smith (1998) found that:

> *A significant minority of Americans resist individual-level privatization. They want religion to speak to social and political issues, and act accordingly. Among religious traditions, conservative movements such as evangelical Protestantism are the most publicly oriented, constituting a reversal of past generations. Liberal Protestants, once the most powerful religious voice in public arenas, are now much more privatized than conservative traditions (p. 1347).*

The Prominence of Evangelicalism

Evangelicalism was effectively shaped by the ideologies of the Third Wave. Shuman and Meador (2003) maintained that evangelicalism in America was shaped by three of the most fundamental tendencies of contemporary North Atlantic culture and its attendant consumer capitalism: radical individualism, narcissism, and therapeutic sensibility. Evangelical Christianity shared many of the values of the Third Wave culture predicted by Toffler, which explained its rise to prominence in American religious life. The success of Evangelicalism may be traced to its adaptation to the Third Wave cultural idioms of consumerism and individualism (Balmer, 2004). Evangelicalism succeeded in the Third Wave because of its adaptability to cultural trends. Balmer (2004) stated:

> *One of the reasons for the success of evangelicalism, if you compare it, say, for example, with mainline Protestantism, is that evangelicalism is always looking for novelty. It's looking for innovation, always looking for the latest edge in communicating to the larger public. In more tradition-bound religious movements, whether it's Presbyterianism or the Episcopal Church or something like that, you have liturgical rubrics, you have centuries or at least decades of tradition, and people are reluctant to countermand that tradition. Evangelicals have no problem with that (p. 2).*

The ideals of evangelicalism attracted working class people once claimed by Second Wave religion. A 1986 pastoral letter from the American Catholic Bishops entitled, *A Pastoral Letter on Economic Justice for All,* stated that labor unions themselves were challenged by the present economic environment to seek new ways of doing business (as reported by Russo & Corbin, 1999). Hicks (2006) recognized that evangelical churches were available for mobilization by Third Wave ideologies because prominent religious pillars of fundamentalist market reform efforts were likely where mobilization by labor unions was weak. In the Third Wave, evangelicalism assumed a new role in filling a void left by Second Wave religion. Straub (2006) noted that:

> *The old interlocking forms of New Deal social democracy — urban machine/social safety net/unionized mass-production industry — are on a terminal slide to extinction. As all over America, they are gradually being replaced by a new comprehensive social organization — nonunion Wal-Mart jobs/antisocial exurban sprawl/hyper-individualist consumerism — whose value system is as oriented towards the Republican right as the old New Deal was to FDR Democrats. In this equation, the role of ideological prime movers has switched: just as left-wing CIO unions used to be the instigators and organizers of the discontent that created the rest of the social structure, now it is the equally (but oppositely) ideological evangelical churches that stoke the fires of blue-collar anger in Ohio. Wal-Mart has replaced the steel companies as the state's largest employer; the sprawling exurbs of Columbus and Cincinnati have replaced Cleveland as its fastest growing areas; and the Assemblies of God and Church of the Nazarene are the new Steelworkers and Autoworkers (p. 2).*

According to Straub, the conservative evangelical movement led to both a growth in adherents and a shift to the right for mainstream Christianity. Straub noted that "…the left has all but abandoned these places where the factories closed and unions died … a right-wing network of churches and businesses offered exactly what the CIO once did: both short-term material gains for members and a militantly transformative vision of the world" (p. 8).

Calsouphes (1998) affirmed that for adults in career transition, the need to be involved in a meaningful activity was strong; Evangelicalism provided the downsized worker the social solidarity that was once characteristic of Second Wave religion and industry. According to Straub (2006), Dana Millbank of the Washington Post said, "...religious conservatives, evangelical churches, have become sort of the new labor unions" (p. 5). The Third Wave transition in American economic and religious life led to the formulation of three primary Third Wave socio-religious values: *individuality, piety,* and *charity*.

Third Wave Religious Attitudes: Individuality-Focused

A social attitude characteristic of the Third Wave society was individualism. Evangelicals largely preach an individual gospel focused on the transformation of individual lives by means of conversion (Penning & Smidt, 2002). In the mid-1980s, 33% of participants told the Gallup Poll that they had been personally born again and by the early 2000s, 46% concurred (as reported by Philips, 2006). Unlike the religion of the Second Wave, the individualistic worldview of evangelicals emphasized that social problems were best addressed by changing individual hearts rather than by reforming social institutions (Penning & Smidt, 2002).

Social struggles in the Third Wave society were conflicts between older community values and newer individualistic values (Russo, 2004). Like the suburbanization of work in the Third Wave, evangelical apologist Guinness recognized that evangelicalism became a "...rather shallow suburban experience" (as reported by

Matzat 1995, p.2). Patterns of evangelical affiliation in the Third Wave were shaped less by the Second Wave ethno-religious patterns of belonging, and more by individuals who decided whether the church was meeting their particular needs or serving them as they wished (Penning & Smidt , 2002).

Third Wave individualism was symbiotically accompanied by consumerism. The consumerism of the Third Wave fed the notion that faith was an individualistic product that was marketed (Budd & Brimlow, 2002). Kale (2004) noted a greater thrust toward the individualization of spirituality among consumers that characterized modern evangelicalism. Unlike the Mainline denominations and Roman Catholicism that dominated the Second Wave, evangelical denominations and independent churches adopted a free market philosophy of church growth: religion of the Third Wave utilized the latest in advertising and marketing techniques to sell religion (Budd & Brimlow, 2002). Most evangelical clergy had the opportunity to effectively market his or her church like an entrepreneur would market a product. In the Third Wave evangelical religion was largely a competitive market segment. Desperation to compete moved the rush to market the faith in the Third Wave (Budd & Brimlow, 2002).

Huntington (1996) noted that as the individualism and consumerism that characterized contemporary evangelicalism spread through a globalized economy, there was almost no resistance in those nations with a Protestant tradition, however, there was some resistance in those with a Roman Catholic tradition. According to Strenski (2004), economic globalization required ideological legitimization and the primary ideologies which informed globalization were explicitly theological. Strenski (2004) maintained that Third Wave globalization retained traces of reliance on its original religious basis. The globalization that characterized the Third Wave was traced to evangelical values. Kurth (1999) noted that globalization, by breaking up and dissolving every traditional, local, and national structure, brought about the universal triumph of expressive individualism (Kurth, 1999). Evangelical religion sanctified market capitalism and raised individualism to theological prominence (Budd & Brimlow, 2002). Evangelicals adopted Third Wave social and economic principles and emerged as the prominent American religious movement of the Third Wave.

Third Wave Religious Attitudes: Charity-Oriented

Evangelicalism adapted to the self-aggrandizement economics of the 1980s, which was why it became so popular during that decade (Balmer, 2004). The emphasis of the dominant individualistic evangelicalism of the Third Wave leaned toward a seductive, commercial gospel in contrast with the social gospel of the Second Wave (Matzat, 1995). Kristin (2005) identified a theology of cosmopolitan consumerism within evangelical culture. The consumerism of free market economics that characterized evangelicalism in the Third Wave distinguished it from the struggles for economic justice of the working class of Mainline Protestantism and Roman Catholicism in the Second Wave.

According to a 2006 *Time Magazine* cover story, 17% of American Christians considered themselves part of the prosperity movement within evangelical Christianity. The prosperity movement emphasized aggressive personal gain as part of God's plan for individual lives, a larger house, more money, and a more expensive car were part of the promises of God (Biema & Chu, 2006). The movement did not characterize all evangelicals and was criticized by megachurch pastors such as Rick Warren, though it represented a growing trend of American evangelicalism descent into full-blown American materialism. Warren noted:

> *When conservative Christianity split from the Mainline in the early 20th century, the latter pursued their commitment to the "social gospel" by working on poverty and other causes such as civil rights and the Vietnam-era peace movement. Evangelicals went the other way: they largely concentrated on issues of individual piety. "We took on personal salvation--we need our sins redeemed, and we need our Savior," But "some people tended to go too individualistic, and justice and righteousness issues were overlooked (as reported by Biema & Chu, 2006, p. 3).*

Similarities existed between the free market economics that characterized the Third Wave and evangelicalism. Evangelicals were historically supportive of laissez-faire welfare policies that left the economic fortune of the poor to a morally bracing market discipline (Hick, 2006). Hilton (1998) indicated that early Victorian evangelicals and utilitarians converged in a belief in individual economic and moral self-reliance, and a kind of institutional laissez-fair of minimal state relief. The ideology of self-reliance corresponded with the evangelical notion of limited institutional mediation of humankind's relation to God (Hilton, 1991). Third Wave consumerism and free market philosophy dictated that the market rewarded and punished the diligent and the indolent; a concept that evangelicalism embraced.

There was a causal impact of late nineteenth century Protestant revivalism upon late nineteenth century Republican voting (Thomas, 1989). The late nineteenth century Evangelicalism was an entrepreneurial middle-class solution to problems of class, legitimacy, and order generated in the early stages of manufacturing (Luebbert, 1991). A pragmatic fusion of religious and free market conservatism marked U.S. conservatism since the 1950s (Diamond, 1995). The resurgence of Evangelicalism took an unusual political turn in the 1980s and dominated American politics (Hammond, 1985). Since the 1990s, white Evangelicals shifted toward laissez-faire views with a shift into Republican partisanship (Hick, 2006). Republicans historically supported free trade, globalization, and other economic philosophies of the Third Wave. Brooks and Manza (2004) noted that white evangelical membership was increasingly composed of Republican partisans; a party that was increasingly broadly anti-redistributive in ideological and policy-making thrusts regarding socioeconomic issues (Poole & Rosenthal, 1997). The alliance between Evangelicalism and the Republican Party demonstrated the ideological fusion of Evangelicalism in the Third Wave.

Consistent with the free market and consumerist ideals of the Third Wave, some early evangelical notions regarding the welfare state included a need for laborers to rely on their own resources and for the nation's governors to hurl away artificial crutches (Mandler, 1990). Philips (2006) noted that economic conservatism found evangelicalism appealing because a preoccupation with otherworldly personal salvation turned lower-income persons away from distracting visions of economic and social reform (Philips, 2006).

According to Green (2004) only 35% of Evangelicals identified welfare and poverty issues as the most significant political priority, compared to 46% of mainline Protestants and 47% of Roman Catholics. Only 43% of Evangelicals agreed that tax dollars should be used to fight poverty, compared to 52% of mainline Protestants and 51% of Roman Catholics.

The Christian Coalition 1995 "Contract with the American Family" called for the enactment of legislation to enhance contributions to private charities as a first step toward transforming the bureaucratic welfare state into a system of private and faith-based compassion charities (as reported by Baltz & Browstein 1996). President of the evangelical ministry, "Focus on the Family", James Dobson, noted that "…social liberals have imposed governmental action, supposedly for the best of motives, but it has had devastating effect" (as reported by Somers & Block 2005, p.266-277). Both groups preferred more charity offered by faith-based organizations and less governmental mediation in matters of economics and social welfare.

Evangelicalism was characterized by a preference for minimal state mediation in matters of social welfare and a preference to allow the market to discipline and reward. Charity emerged from the values of consumerism and free market ideology, which characterized Third Wave religion. The care for individual needs, while allowing for market discipline, set evangelicalism apart from the Second Wave emphasis on social justice. Hexham (2003) noted that evangelicals gave more to charity than members of mainline churches. Charity involved meeting temporary individual needs in an effort to proselytize. Ultimate reform in deindustrialization or other social problems came, according to evangelical theology, not by challenging social structures, but by making converts.

Third Wave Religious Attitudes: Piety-Oriented

The individualistic values of the Second Wave contributed to the evangelical emphasis on personal piety in the Third Wave. Garvey (1993) suggested that Third Wave evangelicalism was singularly characterized by its emphasis on individualistic piety, in contrast with Second Wave religion, which was characterized by an emphasis on community-oriented activism. Underlying evangelical theology was the notion that if enough people were saved, social problems would disappear (Penning & Smidt, 2002).

Similar to the earliest formations of the puritan Protestant ethic, evangelicals Colson and Eckerd (1991) called for religious institutions to preach and teach the work ethic, teach vocation as a divine calling, teach ethics and personal responsibility because a free society depended upon a healthy moral consensus. Piety produced effective individuals able to brace market discipline and emerge as productive and prosperous consumers. Colson and Eckerd maintained that to treat disadvantaged men and women as victims rather than morally responsible individuals only reinforced an expectation of failure. Piety and productivity were thereby tantamount.

Evangelicals of the Third Wave were not socially active in the same way Mainline Protestants and Roman Catholics were socially active in the Second Wave. Thomas (1989) identified a relationship between individualistic religion and individualistic politics. The individualistic emphasis of evangelicalism caused a shift in public concern from that of Second Wave religion. Evangelical appeals in politics were often explicitly moral ones and were often of a popular character with great intensives that reached into people's everyday social lives (as reported by Mann, 1986). Whereas Second Wave religion lobbied for political change in issues of workers' rights, women's rights, and minority rights, Third Wave evangelicalism fought against more personal issues such as abortion, gay marriage, and evolution. The evangelical emphasis on piety was expressed by Witherington (2005) who recognized that when the Ten Commands were taken from the public square, evangelicals felt as though their religious identity was stripped (Witherington, 2005). Evangelicals saw pietistic social issues as moral crises in the American values system, but Toffler (1994) argued that the religion-based wing of the Republican Party, predominantly evangelicals, failed to grasp that the crisis it perceived in the value system reflected the more general crisis of Second Wave civilization as a whole (Toffler, 1994).

The church as a social structure was of marginal importance to Christians in the Third Wave (Budd & Brimlow, 2002). The individualism of evangelical Christianity that characterized the Third Wave was summarized by the perspective of a Youngstown area Assemblies of God clergyman who was quoted in the Youngstown Vindicator after holding a prayer service for workers affected by downsizing. The pastor stated that "...they are not just workers; they are people, and each one has a name". When asked what the pastor's prayer for workers affected by downsizing was, the pastor replied that he hoped the workers would "...learn they can depend on God for their needs, not a corporation" (Youngstown Vindicator, April 6, 2006). Personal responsibility and piety characterized Third Wave evangelical attitudes toward deindustrialization.

Summary of Third Wave Religious Attitudes

Kurth (1999) noted that all revolutions disrupt the traditions and customs and threaten security, safety, and identity. The transition to the Third Wave threatened many economic, social, and religious securities. Without new coalitions and alliances, organized labor, religious institutions, and community groups were marginalized in an increasingly competitive and individualistic society (Russo & Corbin, 1999). The prominence of Evangelicalism in the Third Wave marked new challenges for religious communities confronting the economic and labor issues of 2007 and beyond as Youngstown transitioned out of the Second Wave.

Toffler (1994) maintained that free-marketism and trickle-down twisted into rigid theological dogma were inadequate responses to the Third Wave. As the American economy transitioned out of the Second Wave and into the Third Wave, especially in rustbelt cities like Youngstown, the religious community had a strategic part to play. A shift in economics required a shift in theological perspective from the religious community to determine how to make a demassified society moral and fair (Toffler, 1994). The Third Wave, according to Toffler, demassified culture, values, and morality; Second Wave supporters fought to retain or restore the mass society Third Wave supporters determined how to make de-massification work (Toffler, 1994). In this ideological struggle, religious communities played a significant role in shaping the Third Wave society and the socioeconomic issues surrounding deindustrialization. Though Evangelicalism was the prominent American religion of the Third Wave, its attitudes did not collectively produce the most appropriate response to the labor crises of 2007.

Colson and Eckerd (1991) asserted that when religion spoke on economic issues it usually missed the central message and focused on politics. According to Russo and Corbin (1996), the central question was no longer whether religious communities should respond institutionally, educationally, economically, geographically, and culturally, but rather how social institutions might intervene in more intelligent and supportive ways. In Youngstown a significantly different response from that of the Ecumenical Coalition of 1977 is called for to ensure that the manufacturing crises of 2007 and the transition into the Third Wave will be as smooth as possible.

The Third Wave is a socioeconomic reality in America. The challenge that faced the religious communities of the Mahoning Valley is not a matter of polarization to the political right or left, to the social gospel or evangelical individualism, but to formulate a new comprehensive theology and social action that addressed the moral crises of the Third Wave transition and future economic shifts. The challenge was to preserve the dignity of individuals and meet the human needs presented by corporate downsizing while equally challenging corporations and governments to justice. As Novak (1993) suggested, the ethic proper to political economics is an ethic of prudence, suffused with charity, of justice tempered with mercy. The transition from the Second Wave to the Third Wave requires a calculated religious response of justice and charity, activism and piety, individualism and community.

In the Third Wave the mainline Protestant denominations, Roman Catholics, and Evangelicals have the potential to contribute to the religious response to the Third Wave transition. It will be critical for the religious communities in Youngstown and the Mahoning Valley to work together based on shared concerns for human life, economic justice, and participation in social and religious institutions (Russo & Corbin, 1999) to help the rustbelt community recover from temporary economic crises and progress toward a brighter economic future. Such progress will require a radical change in thinking: a Fourth

Wave social and religious revolution that transforms both religion and society.

CHAPTER 5
Research Findings

An Important Note to the Reader

For those disinterested in the details of the sociological research, feel free to skip this chapter and proceed to the Interpretation of the Research. For those interested in additional detail, the original dissertation is available from University Microfilm/UMI.

Research Hypotheses

The original social research that was conducted investigated how the attitudes of clergy toward deindustrialization in 2007 differed between denominations affiliated with the 1977 Ecumenical Coalition of the Mahoning Valley and denominations that were unaffiliated with the with the 1977 Ecumenical Coalition of the Mahoning Valley. The research, built upon the theoretical framework of the Tofflerian socioeconomic wave model, was designed to investigate clergy attitudes in relation to the economic decline precipitated by deindustrialization in Youngstown. Eight research hypotheses and seven corollary hypotheses were developed and tested:

Hypothesis 1 (H1). Religious Attitudes Toward Deindustrialization second wave subscale values were significantly higher among clergy of denominations that were affiliated with the Ecumenical Coalition of 1977 than among denominations that were unaffiliated with the Coalition.

Hypothesis 2 (H2). Religious Attitudes Toward Deindustrialization third wave subscale values were significantly higher among clergy of denominations that were unaffiliated with the Ecumenical Coalition of 1977 than clergy of denominations that affiliated with the Coalition.

Corollary 2a (C2a). Religious Attitudes Toward Deindustrialization third wave subscale values were significantly higher among clergy of predominantly white-collar congregations than among clergy of predominantly blue-collar congregations.

Hypothesis 3 (H3). Religious Attitudes Toward Deindustrialization justice subscale values were higher among clergy of denominations that were affiliated with the Ecumenical Coalition of 1977 than among clergy of denominations that were unaffiliated with the Coalition.

Corollary 3a (C3a). Religious Attitudes Toward Deindustrialization justice subscale values were higher among clergy of predominantly blue-collar congregations than among clergy of predominantly white-collar congregations.

Corollary 3b (C3b). Religious Attitudes Toward Deindustrialization justice subscale values were higher among clergy who were personally involved in the Ecumenical Coalition of 1977 than among clergy who did not engage in the Ecumenical Coalition of 1977.

Corollary 3c (C3c). There was significant difference in Religious Attitudes Toward Deindustrialization justice subscale values between clergy who served urban churches, suburban churches, and rural churches.

Hypothesis 4 (H4). Religious Attitudes Toward Deindustrialization charity subscale values were significantly higher among clergy of denominations that were unaffiliated with the Ecumenical Coalition of 1977 than among denominations that were unaffiliated with the Coalition.

Corollary 4a (C4a). There was significant difference in the Religious Attitudes Toward Deindustrialization charity subscale values between clergy of congregations that financially supported workers affected by downsizing and clergy who did not financially support workers affected by downsizing.

Corollary 4b (C4b). There was significant difference in Religious Attitudes Toward Deindustrialization charity subscale values between clergy who served urban churches, suburban churches, and rural churches.

Hypothesis 5 (H5). Religious Attitudes Toward Deindustrialization personal piety subscale values were significantly higher among clergy of denominations that were unaffiliated with the Ecumenical Coalition of 1977 than among denominations that were affiliated with the Coalition.

Hypothesis 6 (H6). Religious Attitudes Toward Deindustrialization activism subscale values were higher among clergy of denominations that were affiliated with the Ecumenical Coalition of 1977 than among clergy of denominations that were unaffiliated.

Corollary 6a(C6a). There was significant difference in Religious Attitudes Toward Deindustrialization activism subscale values between clergy who were personally involved in the Ecumenical Coalition of 1977 and clergy who did not engage in the Ecumenical Coalition of 1977.

Hypothesis 7 (H7). Survey of Religious Attitudes Toward deindustrialization community subscale values were higher among clergy of denominations that were affiliated with the Ecumenical Coalition of 1977 than among clergy of denominations that were unaffiliated.

Hypothesis 8 (H8). Religious Attitudes Toward Deindustrialization individuality subscale values were higher among clergy of denominations that were unaffiliated with the Ecumenical Coalition of 1977 than among clergy of denominations that were affiliated with the Coalition.

How the Data was Collected

Much of the detailed research methodology and statistical analysis of the original project was removed for purposes of this book. However, some basic details have been included to explain the methods by which survey data was collected and interpreted. Some details have been included for those interested in social research. The original dissertation is available from University Microfilm/UMI.

The survey contained in the appendix ("Religious Attitudes Toward Deindustrialization) was mailed to the a population of 129 Youngstown area churches. One week after the initial mailing, follow-up phone reminders were made to a random selection of the churches in the population. Two weeks after the initial mailing, surveys were resent to all Roman and Byzantine Catholic churches in the population by the Catholic Diocese of Youngstown using a cover letter from the Executive Director on official diocese stationary. Eleven surveys were promptly returned by Catholic participants.

Participation was solicited by visiting and distributing surveys at the Greater Youngstown Coalition of Christians prayer meeting and the Mahoning Valley Association of Churches ministerium. Most surveys were returned either by fax or in person.

Denominational Representation

Denomination	Number of Responses
Roman Catholic	8
Assembly of God	6
United Methodist	5
Byzantine Catholic	3
American Baptist Churches	2
COGIC	2

Lutheran (ELCA)	2
Presbyterian Church USA	2
Southern Baptist	2
Baptist General Conference	1
Church of God (Cleveland)	1
Disciples of Christ	1
Episcopal	1
Foursquare Gospel	1
Independent	1
Independent Baptist	1
Independent Pentecostal	1

Research Findings Summary

Fifteen hypotheses and corollaries were tested for significance; 11 were tested with a Mann-Whitney U procedure; and four were tested with a Kruskal-Wallis procedure. The null hypotheses were rejected for Corollary 3b and Hypotheses 4, 5, 6, and 7 indicating a significant difference.

Hypothesis Analyses Summary

Hypothesis	Procedure	p or q-Value	Dispositions
H_o1	Mann-Whitney U	.122	Failed to Reject
H_o2	Mann-Whitney U	.730	Failed to Reject
C_o2a	Kruskal-Wallis	.1.176	Failed to Reject
H_o3	Mann-Whitney U	.269	Failed to Reject
C_o3a	Kruskal-Wallis	.435	Failed to Reject
C_o3b	Mann-Whitney U	.043	Null Rejected
C_o3c	Kruskal-Wallis	.948	Failed to Reject
H_o4	Mann-Whitney U	.010	Null Rejected
C_o4a	Mann-Whitney U	.989	Failed to Reject
C_o4b	Kruskal-Wallis	1.482	Failed to Reject
H_o5	Mann-Whitney U	<.001	Null Rejected
H_o6	Mann-Whitney U	.040	Null Rejected
C_o6a	Mann-Whitney U	.102	Failed to Reject
H_o7	Mann-Whitney U	.005	Null Rejected
H_o8	Mann-Whitney U	.066	Failed to Reject

CHAPTER 6
Interpretation of the Research

Research Summary

A survey assessing religious attitudes toward deindustrialization was administered to a population of 129 churches in the city of Youngstown. Forty surveys were completed and returned: Group 1, consisted of 24 clergy from denominations that were affiliated with the Ecumenical Coalition of 1977, and Group 2, consisted of 16 clergy from denominations that were unaffiliated with the Ecumenical Coalition of 1977. The Kruskal-Wallis and Mann-Whitney U procedures were applied to the data to test for significant difference. Conclusions and implications were drawn from the findings of the statistical analysis of the null hypotheses.

Most of the hypotheses proposed by the research were not supported (that is, the null hypotheses were not rejected). Many of the stereotypes proposed by futurists such as Toffler, theologians, and sociologists did not necessarily prove true in Youngstown. An explanation for this phenomenon may be that clergy of Youngstown did not view the problem of deindustrialization in the same way that the literature suggested other religious communities in America viewed similar problems in the past. Several of the hypotheses related to a polarization between mainline Protestants, Roman Catholics, Evangelicals, and Fundamentalists. However, such extreme polarization did not exist among Youngstown clergy. The literature review documented a nationwide stereotype that Evangelicals and Fundamentalists aligned with Third Wave values while Roman Catholics aligned with Second Wave values. Whereas stereotypes may be accurate in the broad culture context of American religion, Youngstown proved to be unique in many ways. An explanation for the variant findings of the research may be attributed to the long struggle for industry between labor and management, private citizens, and local government that characterizes Youngstown's rustbelt image. Perhaps the clergy of Youngstown were not as out of touch as other clergy were nationwide; deindustrialization was a crisis for which the clergy of Youngstown felt intense personal ownership.

A failure to reject the majority of the null hypotheses was a potentially positive outcome to the problem the research addressed. Less significant difference between responses from both clergy from denominations that were affiliated and unaffiliated with the Ecumenical Coalition of 1977 demonstrated that their socioeconomic and theological perspectives were not altogether extreme opposites; at least concerning issues of deindustrialization and corporate downsizing that directly affected Youngstown. Other politicized religious issues may strike more extreme disagreement among the clergy in both groups. However, a genuine concern for Youngstown's economy unifies the clergy, which may be the key to future engagement that leads to genuine transformation and recovery.

Conclusions

Second and Third Wave Socio-economic Values and denominational affiliation

There was no significant difference between Second and Third Wave attitudes toward deindustrialization among the clergy from denominations that were affiliated and unaffiliated with the Ecumenical Coalition of 1977. Lack of significant difference indicated a broad cultural awareness of the diminished role of manufacturing industry and the increased role of technology in 2007. The advent of the Internet and other related technologies was perhaps a contributing factor to a broad awareness of economic shift in America, even for Youngstown, a community slow to recognize economic change and innovation. Even though Second Wave values from clergy of denominations that were affiliated with the Ecumenical Coalition of 1977 were slightly higher than clergy of denominations that were unaffiliated with the Coalition, the difference was observable, but not significant.

Third Wave Values and blue collar and white collar congregations

There was no significant difference between Third Wave attitudes toward deindustrialization among clergy who represented congregations of different employment types. Lack of significant difference indicated that the effects of the Third Wave shift transcended class and other Second Wave structures such as divisions caused by broad unionization. Clergy who served primarily white-collar congregations did not reflect any significantly higher values toward Third Wave concepts than clergy who served primarily blue-collar congregations. Clergy were potentially indifferent to the ideals of the class represented by the congregation in the formation of perspectives on socioeconomic change.

Justice Values and denominational affiliation

There was no significant difference in justice attitudes toward deindustrialization between clergy from denominations that were affiliated and unaffiliated with the Ecumenical Coalition of 1977. Lack of significant difference indicated that the majority of the clergy in Youngstown were concerned about justice for the workforce. Although both groups generally agreed that the Third Wave was a reality and would eventually displace twentieth century industry, the clergy agreed that justice was important to ensure a smooth transition. Further, the clergy agreed that the church should participate in the call for social justice in the community during the period of deindustrialization and economic change.

Justice Values and blue collar and white collar congregations

There was no significant difference between justice attitudes toward deindustrialization among clergy who represented congregations of different employment types. Lack of significant difference indicated that, similar to Third Wave attitudes, concern for justice was not dependent upon the ideals of the class represented by the congregation. Justice was potentially seen as a religious virtue or as a needed perspective for the city of Youngstown in its socioeconomic history.

Justice Values among those who participated in the Ecumenical Coalition of 1977 and those who did not

There was significant difference between justice attitudes toward deindustrialization among the clergy who personally participated in the Ecumenical Coalition of 1977 and those who did not participate in the Coalition. Significant difference indicated that issues of concern from 1977 were not resolved. Although the Ecumenical Coalition was unsuccessful, the values and concerns it represented were still strongly maintained by those who were personally involved.

Justice Values among urban, suburban, and rural congregations

There was no significant difference between justice attitudes toward deindustrialization among clergy who represented congregations of different communities. Lack of significant difference indicated that the urbanization of the Second Wave was no longer a principal factor in the divisions created by broad unionization. Laborers in the Third Wave represented mostly suburban communities. The most significant manufacturing plants in the greater Youngstown area in 2007 were not located in the city limits but in suburban communities.

Charity Values among those who participated in the Ecumenical Coalition of 1977 and those who did not

There was significant difference between charity attitudes toward deindustrialization among the clergy from denominations that were affiliated and unaffiliated with the Ecumenical Coalition of 1977. Significant difference indicated that Third Wave religion maintained charity as an ideal of Christian virtue in addressing social problems. Significant difference indicated that clergy from denominations that were affiliated with the Ecumenical Coalition of 1977 did not value charity as the most effective means by which socioeconomic problems should be addressed by the religious community.

Charity Values among clergy representing congregations that have financially supported workers affected by downsizing and those that have not

There was no significant difference between charity attitudes toward deindustrialization among clergy who represented congregations that financially supported workers affected by downsizing. Lack of significant difference indicated the universality of the awareness of the problem. Even though a congregation may not have financially supported an individual, its clergy recognized the need for the church to do what was reasonably possible to assist families in crisis.

Charity Values among urban, suburban, and rural congregations

There was no significant difference between charity attitudes toward deindustrialization among clergy who represented congregations of different communities. Lack of significant difference indicated that the urban poverty and suburban affluence were no longer defensible dichotomies, when faced with economic crisis. When industry suffered, all communities, both urban and suburban, felt the effects.

Piety Values and denominational affiliation

There was significant difference between piety attitudes toward deindustrialization among the clergy from denominations that were affiliated and unaffiliated with the Ecumenical Coalition of 1977. Significant difference indicated that Third Wave religious values represented an adherence to the Calvinistic-Puritanical ideals of the Protestant Ethic. Piety translated into personal responsibility, self-reliance, and capitalistic economic persuasions. Second Wave religion, on the other hand, did not indicate that issues of piety or morality were relevant to the humanity of the problem.

Activism Values and denominational affiliation

There was significant difference between activism attitudes toward deindustrialization among the clergy from denominations affiliated and unaffiliated with the Ecumenical Coalition of 1977. Significant difference indicated that Second Wave religion valued social activism as an obligation of the religious community. Challenging of structural injustices was, according to clergy from denominations that were affiliated with the Ecumenical Coalition of 1977, a moral ideal relevant to the problem of downsizing. Corporations, management, and government, should be called into account by the religious community.

Activism Values among those who participated in the Ecumenical Coalition of 1977 and those who did not

There was no significant difference between activism attitudes toward deindustrialization among the clergy who personally participated in the Ecumenical Coalition of 1977 and those who did not participate in the Coalition. Lack of significant difference indicated that religious communities in Youngstown have a general concern for challenging social injustice related to economic crisis. Even though the values were generally high, activism values represented by clergy who personally participated in the Ecumenical Coalition of 1977 were not significantly higher than those who did not participate in the Coalition. Perhaps, clergy who participated in the Coalition recognized its failures and did not see social activism as a viable solution for the economic crises of the Third Wave.

Community Values and denominational affiliation

There was significant difference between community attitudes toward deindustrialization among the clergy from denominations that were affiliated and unaffiliated with the Ecumenical Coalition of 1977. Significant difference indicated that Second Wave religion valued the communal aspects of the Christian experience. The value for community of the clergy from denominations that were affiliated with the Ecumenical Coalition of 1977 demonstrated issues of concern such as mutual responsibility, social cohesiveness, and interpersonal sensitivity.

Individuality Values and denominational affiliation

There was significant difference between individuality attitudes toward deindustrialization among the clergy from denominations that were affiliated and unaffiliated with the Ecumenical Coalition of 1977. Significant difference indicated that Second and Third Wave religion both expressed an interest in meeting the needs of the individualistic ideals of Third Wave culture. Although clergy from denominations that were unaffiliated with the Ecumenical Coalition of 1977 expressed observably higher values toward individuality, the difference between the values expressed by clergy from denominations that were affiliated with the Coalition was not significant; perhaps representative of the influence of culture and capitalism on the practice of religion in society.

Implications of the Research

A broad acceptance of Third Wave socioeconomic realities may lead to innovative community development from the religious community and provide new opportunities for social concern beyond polarized political positions that stereotyped Second and Third Wave religion. The acceptance of technology and globalization contributes significant economic awareness in Youngstown if communicated by the clergy. Other Third Wave principles such as individualism, consumerism, and lack of community should be tempered with caution for all denominations and churches. The acceptance of Third Wave values across clergy representing congregations of varying class demonstrated how deep Third Wave values have permeated social structures, transcending Second Wave class divisions. Values once held exclusively by the working class were perhaps abandoned for those of the Third Wave upper-middle class, where materialism, consumerism, and individualism were more prominent.

Because both clergy from denominations that were affiliated and unaffiliated with the Ecumenical Coalition of

1977 generally agreed that justice for workers affected by downsizing was important, new opportunities for dialog may exist. Justice was a value characteristic of Second Wave religion, particularly of the Social Gospel and Catholic Social Teaching movements. In Youngstown, Evangelicals, Fundamentalists, and Independents, representative of Third Wave religion, genuinely cared about how workers were treated as the Third Wave transition occurred. Mutual concern may open the doors of dialog between two groups that have traditionally been in strong political and social disagreement. In like manner, the concern for justice transcended Second Wave class divisions, demonstrating a universal concern from which new opportunities for dialog may develop.

Clergy who participated in the Ecumenical Coalition of 1977, however, had a stronger concern for justice than those who did not participate in the Coalition. Perhaps with new opportunities for innovative dialog, veterans of the cause can inform fellow clergy regarding the mistakes made in the past and provide insight for future efforts. Even though there was a general concern for justice among those who are from denominations that participated in the Ecumenical Coalition of 1977 and those from denominations that did not participate, the clergy who were personally involved in the Coalition offered a unique historical perspective and thereby maintained a stronger concern for justice.

As the manufacturing base moved to suburban locations, the realities of urban industrialism were no longer of grave concern to urban clergy. Issues surrounding manufacturing labor and justice became a suburban problem and the concern was shared among all communities. Because the effects of downsizing touch all communities, another opportunity for dialog emerges.

In step with Calvinistic-Puritanical roots, clergy from denominations unaffiliated with the Ecumenical Coalition of 1977 tended to place a higher value on charity as the means by which religion impacts society; a value that penetrated urban and suburban communities. Dialog should open as to why charity was favored: biblical bases, cultural bases, economic bases? No significant difference of the value of charity between those who financially supported workers affected by downsizing and those who did not financially support workers demonstrated that even though some congregations were not applying charity to the problem, many clergy would support the option should the opportunity present itself. The implementation of charitable programs does not address structural injustice and may only enable immoral action by corporate and government leadership.

Clergy from denominations unaffiliated with the Ecumenical Coalition of 1977 highly valued personal piety, also reinforcing Calvinistic-Puritanical roots. Even though personal piety and responsibility were Christian virtues, they must translate into a social context that is sufficient to address socioeconomic crises such as corporate downsizing and deindustrialization in a concrete and realistic manner.

Significant difference indicated that Second Wave religion, clergy from denominations that were affiliated with the Ecumenical Coalition of 1977, valued social activism as a method by which social change occurs. The polarization between activism and charity represented by the responses of the two groups demonstrated that some stereotypes between mainline Christianity and Evangelicalism were valid. If social activism meant that a political attack on entrenched social evils and structural injustices was the most important part of Christian social life worth considering, it may be inappropriately out of balance and, though well intentioned, may agitate rather than alleviate the problem. The social activism of the Ecumenical Coalition of 1977 represented a failed enterprise of Christian socioeconomic experimentation. If nothing was learned from the mistakes of 1977, a response from the clergy in 2007 and the future will carry the potential for similar failures. However, there was no significant difference for activism values between clergy who personally participated in the Coalition and those who did not participate. Perhaps clergy learned that activism was not the exclusive solution to deindustrialization or other social problems.

Clergy from denominations that were affiliated with the Ecumenical Coalition of 1977 valued community significantly more than clergy from denominations that were unaffiliated with the Coalition. Although both groups generally recognized the reality of the Third Wave, the value of community was still part of the mind of Second Wave clergy. Clergy from denominations that were unaffiliated the Ecumenical Coalition of 1977 expressed observably higher values toward individuality. Personal responsibility and empowerment should not be forfeited for a victim mentality or entitlement, but neither should it be seen as the sole possibility by which social change potentially occurred. The problem of deindustrialization is a community problem, not merely an individual problem, and must be addressed from a community perspective. Not every individual is able to recover easily or entrepreneurially from an economic crisis as significant as regional deindustrialization.

Future Research

Future research may focus on the attitudes of clergy, from denominations that were affiliated with the Ecumenical Coalition of 1977 and those that were unaffiliated, toward a number of critical issues relating to the problem of deindustrialization such as: fair wages for both labor and management, employment security, social welfare, free trade and globalization, community and economic development, community entrepreneurship, retraining, corporate responsibility, or work theology. Demographic data could be collected to determine the number of families affected by downsizing, the number of dollars spent by religious institutions to assist families downsized from manufacturing labor, or how church offerings diminished as an effect of downsizing. Although much data could be gathered and analyzed, it was of utmost importance that the religious community determined its role in society and acted upon it to address socioeconomic crises such as the one faced by Youngstown in 2007 and beyond.

Summary of Research Findings

An explanation of the phenomenology of the research findings was presented, indicating that the stereotypical values represented by the review of literature were not characteristic of the socioeconomic problems posed by deindustrialization in Youngstown. An explanation was given that although theological and political differences often divide the denominational groups dichotomized by the research, clergy in Youngstown uncharacteristically share many of the same concerns for workers and the community.

Eleven conclusions were presented based on the findings derived from statistical analysis of the null hypotheses and corollaries. The most significant conclusions consisted of a failure to reject a null hypothesis related to comparison of the denominational groups dichotomized by the research. Rejection of these hypotheses was based on no significant difference between values expressed by clergy respondents. On theses issues the clergy generally agreed, contrary to the stereotypical divisions often perceived nationwide.

Seven implications were presented based on the conclusions drawn from the statistical analysis of the null hypotheses and corollaries. The most significant implications related to opportunities for dialog between historically divided groups of the religious community. Although some clergy represented denominations that were affiliated with the Ecumenical Coalition of 1977 and others represented denominations that were unaffiliated with the Coalition, common concern was potentially used to develop dialog toward a unified social response to the problems of deindustrialization beyond 2007. Mistakes of the social response of 1977 potentially informed action for a more effective social response in the future.

Future research was proposed in a number of areas including potentially valuable demographic data relating to the role of the religious in deindustrialization and economic recovery. Future research will potentially lead to opportunities for cooperation within the religious community, for clergy of denominations that were affiliated with the Ecumenical Coalition of 1977 and clergy of denominations that were unaffiliated with the Coalition.

CHAPTER 7

Conclusion: The Fourth Wave and Transformational Christianity

An Integrative Social Theology

The emergence of a Fourth Wave economic phenomenon is yet far removed from Youngstown, Ohio. As of 2007, Youngstown faces the difficult transition into the Third Wave economy. However, sociologists and futurologists already predict a Fourth Wave, or quaternary sector of industry comprised of the intellectual services: research, development, and information sciences; services which are emerging from the tertiary sector in some parts of the United States and the world.

The quaternary sector will be the sector in which the economy invests to ensure economic stability, growth and expansion. Research will focus on cost reduction, markets analysis, innovation, and productivity. According to some definitions, the quaternary sector also includes all other pure services, such as entertainment and healthcare.

The notion of a "quinary sector" exists which would encompass preventative health, education, culture and research. Postmodernism and perpetual globalization will continue to erode the values of Second and Third Wave societies.

Although the Youngstown economy may be far from quaternary dominance and further yet from an economy driven by quinary industries, its religious community has a unique opportunity to once again rise to national prominence as active and innovative in response to social change. A Fourth Wave religious movement known as Transformational Christianity may flourish in Youngstown and be a catalyst leading to creative economic and social recovery.

While there remain many apparent ideological differences between the Mainline Protestant, Roman Catholic, and Evangelical/Fundamentalist churches in Youngstown, the concerns that unite the churches may serve as a platform for future dialog and action. The solution for social and economic renewal in Youngstown and other rustbelt cities will not be single-sided; neither the ecumenical nor evangelical ideology has capitalized on the singular solution for social change. While these segments of Christianity have historically polarized over both political and theological issues, common concern for the future of Youngstown's economy may unite the religious community in ways never before imagined. However, true unity will not come in adaptation and compromise; rather, unity will be best achieved through a sincere appreciation of diversity in theology and practice. Movements such as transformationalism and the "emerging church" may bridge the gap between Second and Third Wave ideologies to form a new "Fourth Wave" social theology.

At the peak of the social and political turmoil of the 1960's, theologian Elton Trueblood expressed his concern for what he called a "polarized generation". Trueblood's treatise, *The New Man for Our Time*, speaks quite appropriately and prophetically to the social issues faced by Youngstown and the nation in the midst of Third Wave and post-Third Wave economic and social transition. Trueblood called for a genuine fusion of Christian ideals from both the Mainline Protestants and Roman Catholics and the Evangelicals and Fundamentalists. Trueblood characterized these polarized expressions of Christianity as the "activists and pietists" (both of which were variables assessed in the attitudinal research that was conducted among Youngstown clergy). Trueblood (1970) recognized that both the activist and the pietist have something valuable to contribute to the theological and social conversation:

> *"Much of the sadness of the unhappy conflict in the Church arises from the fact that it is unnecessary. It is logically possible to make one emphasis without, at the same time, denying a contrasting one, providing they are not really contradictory. The important observation to make is that the contrasting insights of the activist and the pietist, far from being contradictory, are really complimentary. The tragedy is that each party is losing something of essential value that it needs for its own authenticity. The merely active person is not truly active, while the merely devout person is not merely*

> *devout. The affirmation of each party is thus ultimately weakened by the character of its denials (p.24)".*

Trueblood did not suggest a compromise of the ideals or emphases of either the activist or pietist; he suggested an integrative fusion of both that compensates for one another's weaknesses and capitalizes one another's strengths. In Trueblood's model, identity is never lost. Trueblood suggested that theological, social, and political polarization produces only "half men [and women] who could be whole men [and women]" (Trueblood, 1970). The wholeness that Trueblood urged was not diplomatic ecumenism, but radical unity that embraces and welcomes diversity as an empowering strength, not a debilitating weakness. Polarization is representative of the Second and Third Wave religious and social dominance that historically stifled growth and recovery in Youngstown. In *One Dimensional Man: Studies in the Ideology of Advanced Industrial Society*, Marcuse (1964) likewise noted a coming of age of industrial society that was characterized by a "marked unification or convergence of opposites" that would bear upon the very possibilities of social change.

While the research identified that a rift of attitudes toward community and individuality exists among the Youngstown clergy, Trueblood denounced the "supposed necessity of choosing between the needs of the individual and the needs of society" (Trueblood, 1970). The transformation of individuals and the transformation of society, Trueblood argued, are inextricably interdependent. Quoting George Buttrick, Trueblood stated: "If religion does not begin with the individual it never begins; but if it ends with the individual – it ends!"

(Trueblood, 1970). A genuine renewal of the society and economy of Youngstown will never be accomplished by either the activists (Mainline Protestants and Roman Catholics) or the pietists (Evangelicals and Fundamentalists) if each insists on working independently of the other. Radical interdependence, as Trueblood called for more than 30 years ago, is the only solution that will genuinely transform the city.

Transformational Christianity

Trueblood's expression of wholistic Christian mission is being worked out by a 21st Century (or Fourth Wave) movement known as Transformational Christianity. Transformationalism is a budding movement within American religious community. Transformationalism represents a fusion of Evangelicalism, Pentecostalism, and Mainline Ecumenicalism. Unlike the sectarian units by which it is comprised, transformationalism is typically embodied in regional "meta-church" alliances: churches from different denominations rather than polarized churches, denominations, or parachurch organizations. Unlike ecumenism, transformationalism is not an expression of denominational uniformity, but an expression of interdenominational alliances. The research indicated that on most issues relating to deindustrialization, Youngstown clergy are largely in agreement. Broad social concern for justice in Youngstown's economy and workforce among diverse religious groups may lead recovery in Youngstown to be an ideal experiment in transformational theology and praxis. While some forms of transformationalism are sensationalized, the general principles may prove useful to economic and social recovery in Youngstown.

Transformational thought emerged from a series of unrelated city-wide revivals that occurred in the 1990s. George Otis, Jr. presented a popular yet suspicious film entitled *Transformations* and Jack Dennison authored *City Reaching*; together their work popularized the basic concepts embodied in transformationalism. The concept of "marketplace ministry" was likewise promoted by Argentinian evangelist Ed Silvoso in his book *Anointed for Business*,. Silvoso introduced the concept of "marketplace transformation" and elaborated the concept of "marketplace ministry".

Transformationalists typically involve a cooperative movement among Catholic, Protestant, and Evangelical churches. Transformationalists are mostly found among evangelicals, however, they are generally more concerned with inclusiveness than exclusivity, and are willing to work with more progressive theological views if a compatible vision of the goals and means of social transformation is shared. Transformational movements are often mediated by other transdenominational initiatives such as the Alpha Course or Promise Keepers, both of which share an interdenominational emphasis and ecumenical spirit.

In mid-2004, the first conferences on Transformation were announced, for 2005 in Indonesia and 2007 in Seoul, Korea. The conferences focus on five "streams" of transformation: church planting, revival, reaching cities, marketplace ministry, and economic development for the poor. The goal is to develop a transformational covenant to provide further definition to the movement.

Transformational Christianity interprets the gospel from a unified perspective of transforming individuals and interpersonal relations and as well as social structures and institutions. The emphasis of transformational praxis is less on theological or political correctness than on effective transformation of society. Transformationalism reflects "kingdom theology" and the "radical middle" approach to Christianity proposed by Gordon Fee, which characterized the role of the church as manifesting God's kingdom on earth. Similar to Fee's approach, Vineyard historian Bill Jackson expressed the need for a less polarized approach between Charismatics and Evangelicals in his book *The Quest for the Radical Middle*.

In the Oxford Centre for World Missions review of the book *Mission as Transformation: A Theology for the Whole Gospel* by Samuel and Sugden (1999), Myers (nd) promoted a "biblical view of mission in which God calls all human beings to love God and their neighbor; never creating a separation between the two". The grounding premise of transformationalism, the concept of commitment to God and neighbor inextricably interdependent, is precisely the theological revolution Trueblood called for in *The New Man for Our Time*.

A Statement from the Lausanne Covenant

The Lausanne Covenant is a 1974 manifesto promoting active world-wide Christian evangelism. One of the most influential documents in modern Evangelical Christianity, it was written and adopted by 2,300 evangelicals at the International Congress on World Evangelization in Lausanne, Switzerland. The covenant is in the form of an ecumenical confession. While the covenant was written primarily by Evangelicals, its definition of transformation is useful to the future of the city of Youngstown:

> *"Transformation is the progressive and ongoing, measurable, supernatural impact of the presence and power of God working in, through, and apart from the Church on human society and structures. In the Church, this is characterized by increased holiness of life, reconciliation in relationships, and appetite for prayer and worship. Through the Church, this is characterized by accelerated conversion growth, mobilization of gifts and callings, and an increased relevance to and participation in greater society. In the culture, this may be characterized by pervasive awareness of the reality of God, a radical correction of social ills, a commensurate decrease in crime rates, supernatural blessing of local commerce, healing of the brokenhearted (the alienated and disenfranchised), regenerative acts of restoring the productivity of the land, exporting of kingdom righteousness (Lausanne, 1974)."*

The statement is appreciable not only by Evangelicals, but by the broad spectrum of the Church. The call to action of the Lausanne Covenant may be championed by diverse segments within the Church based on respective social and spiritual strengths and ideals. The majority of statements in the Lausanne definition of transformation could be easily embraced somewhere along the dialectical spectrum proposed later in this chapter.

Transformationalism is similar to the "empowered evangelicalism" claimed by the Vineyard movement, from which much of its inspiration was arguably drawn. The Vineyard emphasis has been an evangelical social theology of the kingdom of God: now but not yet, present, but future. By shifting the focus to broad social transformation rather than individual conversions, transformationalism is adopting many of the social-involvement techniques and approaches of Mainline Christianity as opposed to the more confrontational approach of Fundamentalism. Thus, transformationalism represents the fusion of the personal engagement of Evangelicalism and the structural engagement of the Social Gospel. Transformationalism effectively represents a synthesis of two seemingly opposing philosophies of social change. The synthesis is representative of three basic components of transformational thought: missional living, marketplace ministry, and the church of the locality.

Missional Living

The terms "missional" and "missional living" originated in the work of a group of North America practitioners, missiologists and theorists, called the *Gospel and Our Culture Network (GOCN)* to give definition to the life and work of the missionary thinker Lesslie Newbigin. After returning from a lifetime of work as a missionary in India, Newbigin was startled by his perception of a paganized Western civilization. Newbigin articulated the view that the Western world was a mission field that required a missiology relevant to the culture.

Kimball (2003) noted that the average church "focuses most efforts on the quality of the programs and ministries to keep those already attending happy rather than on [a] biblical mission". Kimball asserted that this preoccupation led to a "narrowed the definition of the church as a 'place where' instead of a 'people who are'" (p.92). Further, Kimball argued that in a postmodern context, people won't "go to church" but will "be the church on a mission together" (p.95). The concept of missional living radically merges the propositional nature of Evangelical Christianity, the social nature of Mainline Christianity, and the sacramental nature of Roman Catholicism into a mission-oriented praxis for transformational change.

McLaren (2004) defined missional living as the goal to "inflict less damage and more blessing on the world" in a way that universally brings "good news to Christians and non-Christians alike" (pp.119-120). McLaren argued that should Christians choose to live missionally, the postmodern world would not wallow in Second or Third Wave principles, but could witness genuine recovery in all aspects of public and private life. The effects of transformational and missional Christianity were expressed by McLaren as follows:

> *"Even if only a few people would practice this new way, many would benefit. Oppressed people would be free. Poor people would be liberated from poverty. Minorities would be treated with respect. Sinners would be loved, not resented. Industrialists would realize that God cares*

> *for sparrows and wildflowers -- so their industries should respect, not rape, the environment. The homeless would be invited in for a hot meal. The kingdom of God would come – not everywhere at once, not suddenly, but gradually, like a seed growing in a field, like yeast spreading in a lump of bread dough, like light spreading across the sky at dawn (p.121-122)".*

While McLaren's view may seem idealistic, it is less idealistic than was the Social Gospel and more aligned with Niebuhr's social realism. Missional living is not bewitched by what Tournier (1964) called the "naïve confidence in progress of man" (p.123). Missional living does not set out to achieve the impossible, but to simply live all that is possible in every aspect of social life.

It should be noted that some extreme expressions of transformationalism borrow theological ideas from the Latter Rain Movement, Manifest Sons of God, and Kingdom Now theology. Similar to the Social Gospel, Kingdom Now theology and related movements emphasize the possibility of a Christianized society that is just and prosperous where laws that reflect enforced biblical ideals. However, more realistic transformationalism emphasizes that humble service and a commitment to the common good, rather than political maneuvering, leads to genuine social change. Sensational expressions and unrealistic expectations for transformational theology and practice should soberly consider Bergon's warning that "humanity groans, half crushed under the progress it has made" (Tournier, 1969). Transformational renewal is possible but utopia is not.

True and realistic missional living simply emphasizes a community of God's people defined and organized by God's mission to the world. According to the missional definition, the Church's true and authentic organizing principle is mission. When the church is in mission, it is the true Church. The mission of God (*missio dei*) flows directly through every individual and every community of faith in communion with that mission. The mission can express itself in the myriad ways in which the kingdom of God expresses itself: diverse and redemptive. The mission, perhaps defined differently by different churches, is still always unified by the principles of diversity and redemption. For a city like Youngstown, a realization of mission would mean social, economic, and spiritual transformation for the individuals and structures of the city and region.

Marketplace Ministry

Once chaplain to the United States Senate Richard Halverson (1916-1995) authored a little known book simply entitled *Relevance*. In the book, Halverson accused the church of being obsessed with preserving institutionalization and void of real social influence. Halverson challenged churches, and individual Christians, to become "benevolent infectors" in society through a "ministry of anonymity" (Halverson, 1968). The convictions Halverson presented were very much in alignment with the postmodern concept of missional living, though he wrote at the peak of modernity (Second Wave). In more ways than one, Halverson was a prophetic voice of his generation. Halverson (1968) proposed two simple questions, each with potentially irrelevant and relevant answers: where is your church and what does your church do? The irrelevant and conventional responses are, for the first question, the street address of the church, and for the second question, a list of worship services and programs. However, Halverson's proposed answers are far more missional and transformational:

> *"But what ought the answers to those questions be? (1) 'Where is your church?' Answer: 'All over the metropolitan [area], in about three hundred homes and apartments, in schools and clubs, in markets and offices ... (2) 'What does your church do?' Answer: 'Many things. She keeps house, teaches school; sells groceries and hardware, clothing and cars, insurance and appliances. She practices law and medicine and dentistry. She makes laws and serves in the military --- constructs highways and buildings --- serves our government overseas in embassies, in Peace Corps, and in foreign aid programs. Our church is everywhere, in everything, doing everything that needs to be done for the sake of Christ and for the glory of God." (Halverson, 1968, pp.77-78).*

Religious public servants such as Halverson with incredible social insight set the stage for what the transformational movement calls "marketplace ministry". The term "marketplace" indicates the secular world; that is, industry, business, education, and government. Marketplace ministers do not perform within the conventional context of the church, the role historically championed by religious workers to whom Halverson referred as "an island of irrelevant piety" (Halverson, 1968). Marketplace ministers succeed in business and government with innovation, increased profits, efficiency, and team-oriented people building. The emphasis for transformational marketplace ministers is not to proselytize, but to make the marketplace better for Christians and non-Christians alike. The transformational ministry of economic reconciliation is for justice and prosperity for all. Marketplace ministers are not simply called to financially prosper to funnel money into church-related programs or even to recruit people into the church; rather, they are seen by transformationalism as the primary carriers of the kingdom of God in the world. Marketplace ministers are a Fourth Wave fusion of missional living and Halverson's "benevolent infectors".

Marketplace ministry is implementation of the Reformation emphasis on the "priesthood of all believers"; a blurring of lines between clergy and laity. However, marketplace ministry should be distinguished from Weber's Protestant Ethic, which emphasized personal prosperity as testimony to piety. Transformationalism affirms the intrinsic value of work, both as an aspect of worship and as a service to society, recognizing the challenges of post-modernism and the post-Christian culture. The end-goal of marketplace ministry is not to make converts, but to manifest the kingdom of God in the workplace.

The Church of the Locality

Another concept often unique to transformationalism is the innovation of city-wide churches. While most Christians affirm the concepts of one "Church universal" and simultaneously many "local congregations", transformationalism promotes the concept of a third, intermediate tier: "the "church of the region" or the "city church". The city church comprises all of the local congregations in a particular region, regardless of denominational affiliation, as vital components of a single, unified church family. United, the regional churches think, plan, and serve together under a common missional framework. The concept of the church of the region does not impose a single uniform structure. Rather, it involves formalizing the existing networks of relationship and trust into a fluid organizational structure, usually involving councils of recognized leaders from different faith communities.

This typically means the church as a whole develops a common vision, which is implemented by individual congregations with minimal explicit coordination. The city-church model also enables the Christian community to speak with one voice when dealing with local government; however, the focus is usually on finding ways to cooperate in serving the community rather than dictating public policy or a uniform ecclesiology.

The concept of the city-church may serve Youngstown well as steps are taken by the religious community toward economic and social recovery. The transformational city church extends beyond ecumenism and invites Evangelicals and Fundementalists to finds their place at the table. Unlike the Ecumenical Coalition of the Mahoning Valley in 1977, the city-church concept may attract those who abstained from prior involvement. The city church need not look nor function like ecumenism; rather, it can serve a transformational purpose that attracts broader participation.

A Model for Transformational Christianity

The following model represents a theological dialectic (according to the philosopher/theologian Hegel, the development of one idea or condition into another by the process of thesis, antithesis and synthesis) for transformation. The dialectic is a tool that emerged from the research conducted on the socioeconomic attitudes of Youngstown clergy and the ideals of Trueblood's clarion call to wholeness, Halverson's concept of the ministry of anonymity, and the grounding ideologies of transformationalism.

Because the model is dialectical, it does not depend upon the logical premise of *either/or* but of *both/and*. Should an individual express an imbalanced strength on either side of the model, it does not suggest incorrectness or inherent fault. Rather, it represents the opportunity for expression of values somewhere between two seemingly polarized extremes. The thesis and antithesis therefore become for each individual, church, and denomination, a synthesis. The goal of the dialectic is to serve as a tool or a paradigm, through which the social problems faced by Youngstown can be viewed to engage wide and diverse participation of area churches.

A Theological Dialectic for Transformation
A Synthesis of Matthew 22:37-40 and Micah 6:8

Social Transformation (Activism)	Personal Transformation (Piety)
Love others unconditionally.	Love God completely.
Do justice and love kindness.	Walk humbly with your God.

©2007 JDR

The dialectic provides a way for Youngstown clergy and laity to better understand one another. Some clergy from the Mainline churches may be strong on the side of social transformation (activism) while other clergy from Evangelical churches may be strong on the side of personal transformation (pietism). The apparent gap between the values should not polarize but unify. In the transformational model, an over-expression in either extreme does not indicate failure, but a constructive contribution at once to God's kingdom and to all of secular society. The ideal of the dialectic is not to attempt a balancing act, but to work effectively together in unified diversity.

The dialectic represents a synthesis of the command of Jesus in Matthew 22:37-40 to "love the Lord your God" and "love your neighbor as yourself", as well as the classic simplification of "what is good" from Micah 6:8. The dialectic is not intended to be a comprehensive theology and certainly not a proper exegesis. However, the plain reading and application of the scripture in these two cases make the model useful to Mainline Protestants, Roman Catholics, and Evangelicals alike. If universal aspects of the faith, what Trueblood called the "roots", are genuinely lived by clergy and laity alike, the "fruits" will most certainly be consequentially present (Trueblood, 1970). The results of the conducted research should produce a spirit of unity among churches in the Youngstown area that leads to a transformational vision for the future; economic and social renewal will follow.

The dialectic is also generally representative of both Mainline Protestant/Roman Catholic and Evangelical/Fundamentalist approaches to social change. The approaches may be illustrated with vertical lines set parallel to one another:

Two Approaches to Social Change

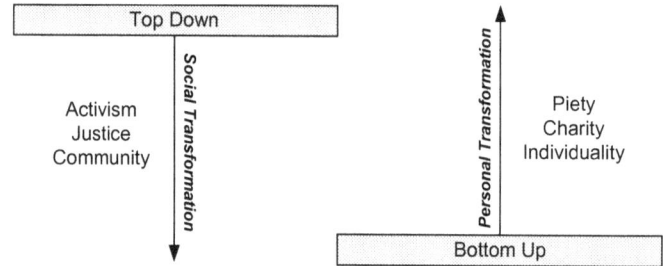

Mainline Protestants, hailing from the Social Gospel Tradition, and Roman Catholics, hailing from the Catholic Social Teaching tradition, approach social change from the top down. That is, structural change must be achieved in order for individual change to occur. The top-down approach is representative of the Second Wave values of the research: activism, justice, and community.

Evangelicals and fundamentalists, with more puritanical and Calvinistic roots, approach social change from the bottom up. That is, personal change must be achieved in order for structural change to occur. The bottom-up approach is representative of the Third Wave values of the research: piety, charity, and individuality.

From a macro-level perspective, it is not difficult to see the dialectic at work in both approaches to social change. While one perspective prefers to work from the bottom up, changing individual lives and redirecting souls, the other perspective prefers to work from the top down, changing social institutions and lobbying for justice. With a simple rearrangement of the diagram, the two perspectives, so often stereotyped as incompatible opposites, converge in the middle at some agreeable goal. The meeting point of both approaches is the socio-religious goal toward which transformationalism is striving:

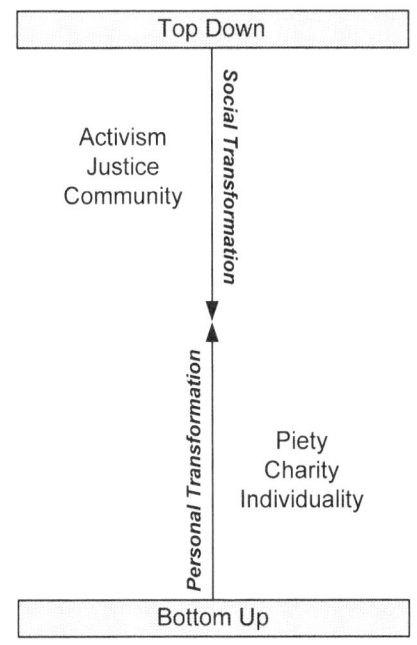

Conclusion: Application and Action

Theory and theology are impotent without very real praxis. The dialectic presented in this chapter may serve to engage the churches of Youngstown in new dialog that leads to corresponding action in the community. Christians may learn to be better people or more pious, society may become a little more just, but ultimately action must translate into sustainable goals that provide an economic and social hope for Youngstown's future.

One example of realistic application of the research and the dialectic could be as follows:

The research indicated that:

1. For the most part, the clergy of Youngstown recognized that the American economy is changing: giving way to Third Wave (and soon Fourth Wave) economic trends such as a globalization, consumerism, and high-technology.
2. The clergy of Youngstown are in general agreement that justice is an important issue for workers affected by deindustrialization and corporate downsizing. Justice means more than charity: it means real action that leads to sustaining or creating reliable jobs and economic vitality while calling corporations and government to account.

The dialectic suggests that:

3. Approaches to achieve change in Youngstown need not be polarized. It is possible to approach Youngstown's social and economic crises related to

deindustrialization with a humble acquiescence of "both and" rather than "either or".
4. Mainline Protestants, Roman Catholics, Evangelicals, and Fundamentalists will each approach the problems of Youngstown differently. Each stream of Christianity will experience a unique biblical, spiritual, and historical call to action according to the respective tradition. The difference of approach does not negate or invalidate other approaches.

The following questions may open dialog:

5. How will the pietists approach the issue of justice for workers affected by corporate downsizing? What does a bottom-up approach look like? How is "loving God" responsive to the problem? How will humility contribute to a solution? Which pietistic practices should be engaged? How does charity lead to justice? What does justice for the individual look like?
6. How will the activists approach the issue of justice for workers affected by corporate downsizing? What does a top-down approach look like? How is "loving the neighbor" responsive to the problem? How should mercy and justice be exhibited? What social action can be implemented? What does justice for the community look like?

This systematic approach to tackling the difficult socio-economic issues faced by Youngstown may assist the clergy in opening dialog where theological and social differences previously inhibited any joint discussion. However, dialog must be translated into real action. Real policies, prayers, protests, and pastoral care must emerge. Statistics and theories are only means to an end.

The research presented in this book and its interpretation may serve as a valuable tool for the clergy of Youngstown if taken seriously and acted upon. Economic vitality is not an unrealistic goal. Change is possible. Perhaps 30 years from now, when the next book on religion and industry is written about Youngstown, the city may be remembered not as a tragedy of deindustrialization, but as a city whose churches never gave up on its potential and its people: a city where a relentless commitment to genuine social and economic transformation turned rust into renewal.

APPENDIX
Survey Utilized by the Research

FORM-M

Please answer the following questions. Choose only one response when responses are provided.

Name of Church:	
Denominational Affiliation (Please be specific):	
Gender:	☐ Male ☐ Female
What is your age?	_____
What is your Seminary Education?	☐ 4-year college ☐ Seminary/Graduate School ☐ Diploma/Certificate ☐ Informal Training/Other
What type of community does your church serve?	☐ Urban ☐ Suburban ☐ Rural
How would you describe the ethnicity of your congregation?	☐ Primarily African American ☐ Primarily Latino ☐ Primarily Caucasian ☐ Multicultural
How would you describe the employment of your congregation?	☐ Primarily Blue Collar ☐ Primarily White Collar ☐ Primarily Unemployed
Were you directly involved with the Ecumenical Coalition of the Mahoning Valley during the 1977 steel crisis?	☐ Yes ☐ No
Has your church financially supported a family from your congregation who was downsized from manufacturing labor?	☐ Yes If yes, how many? _____ ☐ No

Please answer the following questions to the best of your ability. Circle the number that best reflects your agreement or disagreement with each statement. By circling "1" you strongly disagree with the statement. By circling "10" you strongly agree with the statement.

1. The religious community should be politically involved in socioeconomic issues.

1	2	3	4	5	6	7	8	9	10
Strongly Disagree									Strongly Agree

2. Churches should care for the needs of workers affected by downsizing before unemployment insurance or government assistance is provided.

1	2	3	4	5	6	7	8	9	10
Strongly Disagree									Strongly Agree

3. The Christian Faith is more of a community experience than an individual conversion.

1	2	3	4	5	6	7	8	9	10
Strongly Disagree									Strongly Agree

4. Consumer credit is the best way for individuals to live a more comfortable lifestyle.

1	2	3	4	5	6	7	8	9	10
Strongly Disagree									Strongly Agree

5. It is immoral to replace the positions of unskilled American laborers with cheaper foreign labor.

1	2	3	4	5	6	7	8	9	10
Strongly Disagree									Strongly Agree

6. The poor choices of individuals are more to blame for poverty than social injustice.

1	2	3	4	5	6	7	8	9	10
Strongly Disagree									Strongly Agree

7. Outsourcing of American manufacturing jobs is hurting the American economy.

1	2	3	4	5	6	7	8	9	10
Strongly Disagree									Strongly Agree

14. A free market will reward with prosperity those who are diligent and punish with poverty those who are not.

1	2	3	4	5	6	7	8	9	10
Strongly Disagree									Strongly Agree

15. The current wave of industrial downsizing is only a temporary economic anomaly. Manufacturing industry in Northeast Ohio and Western Pennsylvania is here to stay.

1	2	3	4	5	6	7	8	9	10
Strongly Disagree									Strongly Agree

16. Technology should replace jobs once performed by laborers.

1	2	3	4	5	6	7	8	9	10
Strongly Disagree									Strongly Agree

17. Social problems can be resolved by the religious community publicly challenging structural injustices in society.

1	2	3	4	5	6	7	8	9	10
Strongly Disagree									Strongly Agree

18. Religion has more of an obligation to care for the poor of a community than to fight for social change.

1	2	3	4	5	6	7	8	9	10
Strongly Disagree									Strongly Agree

19. Christianity is more about loving our neighbor than personal holiness.

1	2	3	4	5	6	7	8	9	10
Strongly Disagree									Strongly Agree

20. It is the responsibility of workers affected by downsizing to find retraining for new jobs on their own.

1	2	3	4	5	6	7	8	9	10
Strongly Disagree									Strongly Agree

21. Some injustices in society are beyond the control of individuals and their personal decisions.

1	2	3	4	5	6	7	8	9	10
Strongly Disagree									Strongly Agree

22. Moral issues such as gay marriage and abortion are more politically important than minimum wage law and social security.

1	2	3	4	5	6	7	8	9	10
Strongly Disagree									Strongly Agree

23. Labor unions are an essential part of twenty first century economics and business practices.

1	2	3	4	5	6	7	8	9	10
Strongly Disagree									Strongly Agree

24. Without a college education, it is difficult to succeed in the twenty first century workforce.

1	2	3	4	5	6	7	8	9	10
Strongly Disagree									Strongly Agree

25. Religious institutions should be directly involved in government-funded community and economic development programs.

1	2	3	4	5	6	7	8	9	10
Strongly Disagree									Strongly Agree

26. The most a church can do to help workers affected by downsizing is to meet their immediate physical needs during unemployment.

1	2	3	4	5	6	7	8	9	10
Strongly Disagree									Strongly Agree

27. Christianity should be more concerned with the common good than with individual needs.

1	2	3	4	5	6	7	8	9	10
Strongly Disagree									Strongly Agree

28. Individuals should choose a church because it meets their individual needs, not because it is in their immediate community.

1	2	3	4	5	6	7	8	9	10
Strongly Disagree									Strongly Agree

29. Unskilled American laborers are treated poorly by corporations.

1	2	3	4	5	6	7	8	9	10
Strongly Disagree									Strongly Agree

30. The eternal destination/afterlife of an individual is more important than the quality of his or her life on earth.

1	2	3	4	5	6	7	8	9	10
Strongly Disagree									Strongly Agree

31. Manufacturing jobs will someday be the predominant type of employment in the Mahoning Valley once again.

1	2	3	4	5	6	7	8	9	10
Strongly Disagree									Strongly Agree

32. The workforce of the past was less-skilled than the workforce of the future.

1	2	3	4	5	6	7	8	9	10
Strongly Disagree									Strongly Agree

END OF SURVEY.
THANK YOU FOR YOUR PARTICIPATION!

TO RETURN SURVEY, PLEASE FAX (TOLL-FREE) TO: 1-877-838-9162

Bibliography

Works Cited

Abell, A. (1968). *American catholic thought on social questions.* Indianapolis, IN: Bobbs-Merill.

Balmer, R. (2004, May 7). Interview with Randall Balmer: Evangelicals and evangelism. Religion and Ethic Weekly. Retrieved on June 23, 2006, from http://www.pbs.org/wnet/religionandethics/week736/interview.html

Baltz, D. & Brownstein, R. (1996). *Storming the gates: Protest politics and the republican.* Revival, Boston: Little, Brown, and Company.

Biema, D & Chu, J. (2006, September 11). Does God want you to be rich? *Time,* Retrieved on October 31, 2006 from http://www.time.com/time/magazine/article/0,9171,1533448,00.html

Blackburn, R. (1997). The reproduction of social inequality. *Sociology, 31(3),* 491-509.

Budde, M. & Brimlow, R. (2002). *Christianity incorporated.* Grand Rapids, MI: Brazos Press.

Buss, T. (1983). *Shutdown at Youngstown: Public policy for mass unemployment.* Albany, NY : State University of New York Press.

Calsouphes, C. (1998). An exploration of the internal experience of career-related transitions in mid-life. (Doctoral dissertation, Harvard University, 1998).

Carlaw, K. & Lipsey, R. (2003). Productivity, technology and economic growth: What is the relationship? *Journal of Economic Surveys, 17,* 457-495.

Cetron, M. & Davies, O. (2005, May-June). Technology trends. *The Futurist.*

Collins, K. (2005). *The Evangelical moment: The promise of an American religion.* Grand Rapids, MI: Baker Academic.

Colson, C. & Eckerd, J. (1991). *Why America doesn't work: How the decline of the work ethic is hurting your family and future and what you can do.* Dallas, TX: Word Publishing.

Diamond, P. (1995). Virtue and the promise of conservatism: The legacy of Burke and Tocqueville. *The Journal of Politics,* 57(3).

Dobbs, L. (2004). *Exporting America: Why corporate greed is shipping American jobs overseas.* New York, NY: Warner Business Books.

DOLETA: US Department of Labor Employment and Training Administration (n.d.). *Fact Sheet: The worker adjustment and retraining notification act: A guide to advance notice of closings and layoffs.* Retrieved October 23, 2006, from http://www.doleta.gov/programs/factsht/warn.htm

Ebberwein, C. (2000). Adaptability and the characteristics necessary for managing adult career transition: A qualitative investigation. (Doctoral dissertation, University of Kansas, 2000).

Eckel, E. (1920). *Coal, iron, and war.* New York, NY: Henry Holt.

Ewald, K. (2004). The graying of the Ohio labor force. Columbus, OH: Ohio Bureau of Labor Market Information/Office of Workforce Development. Retrieved on August 1, 2006, from http://lmi.state.oh.us/research/GrayingOhioLaborForce.pdf

Frank, T. (2000, October 30). The rise of market populism. *The Nation.* Retrieved on August 15, 2006 from http://www.thenation.com/docprint.mhtml?i=20001030&s=frank

Fuechtmann, T. (1989). *Steeples and stacks: Religion and steel crisis in Youngstown, Ohio.* Cambridge, MA: Cambridge University Press.

Gardner, C. (1914). *The ethics of Jesus and social progress.* New York, NY: George H. Doran Company.

Garvey, J. (1993). *Fundamentalisms and the state: Remaking polities, economies, and militancy.* Chicago, IL: University of Chicago Press.

Green, J. (2004). *The American religious landscape and political attitudes: A baseline for 2004.* Akron, OH: University of Akron. Retrieved on September 3, 2006, from http://pewforum.org/publications/surveys/green-full.pdf

Halverson, R. (1968). *Relevance.* Waco, TX: Word Books.

Hammond, P. (1985). The curious path of conservative Protestantism: Annals of the American academy of political and social science. *Religion in America Today,* 480.

Handy, R. (1949). The Influence of Mazzini on the American Social Gospel. *The Journal of Religion, 29*(2).

Handy, R. (1960). The American religious depression:1925-1935. *Church History, 29*(1).

Hexam, I. (1993). *The growth of conservative Evangelical religion.* University of Alberta: Calgary, AB. Retrieved on October 12, 2006, from http://www.acs.ucalgary.ca/~nurelweb/papers/irving/TEDHEW.html

Hill, E. (2001). Ohio's competitive advantage: Manufacturing productivity. Maxine Goodman Levin College of Urban Affairs of Cleveland State University. Retrieved July 12, 2006, from http://urban.csuohio.edu/research/ohiomanufacturing.htm

Hilton, B. (1998). *The age of atonement: The influence of Evangelicalism on social and economic thought.* Clarendon, UK: Oxford.

Hira, R. & Hira, A. (2005). *Outsourcing America: What's behind our national crisis and how we can reclaim American jobs.* New York, NY: American Management Association.

Huntington, S. (1996). The clash of civilizations and the remaking of world order. London, UK: Simon & Schuster.

Johnson, B. (1982). Taking stock: Reflections on the end of another era. *Journal for the Scientific Study of Religion, 21*(3).

Johnson, D. (1973). Between evangelicalism and a social gospel: The case of Joseph Rayner Stephens. *Church History, 42*(2).

Kale, S. (2004). Spirituality, religion, and globalization. *Journal of Macromarketing, 24*(2), 92-107.

Kimball, C. (2002). *When religion becomes evil.* New York, NY: Harper Collins.

Kimball, D. (2003). *The emerging church.* Grand Rapids, MI: Zondervan.

King, W. (1981). The emergence of social gospel radicalism: The Methodist case. *Church History, 50*(4).

Kurth, J. (1999). Religion and globalization. *The Templeton lecture on religion and world affairs, 7*(7).

Lane, D. (1976). *The socialist industrial state: towards a political sociology of state socialism.* Boulder, CO: Westview Press.

Leo XIII (1891, May 15). *On the condition of the working classes: Rerum novarum.* Encyclical letter. Retrieved on August 22, 2006, from http://www.vatican.va/holy_father/leo_xiii/encyclicals/documents/hf_l-xiii_enc_15051891_rerum-novarum_en.html

Luebbert, G. (1991). *Liberalism, fascism, or social democracy.* New York, NY: Oxford University Press.

Mandler, P., 1990. *Aristocratic government in the age of reform.* New York, NY: Oxford University Press.

Mann, Catherine (2003, December). *Globalization of IT services and white collar jobs: The next wave of productivity growth.* Washington, DC: The Institute for International Economics PB03-11.

Mathews, Y. (1927). The development of social Christianity in America during the past twenty-five years. *Journal of Religion, 7*(4).

Matzat, D. (1995). The corruption of modern evangelicalism. *Issues Etc. Journal, 1*(1).

McKinsey Global Institute (2003). *Offshoring: Is it a win-win game?* San Francisco, CA.

McLaren, B. (2004). *A generous orthodoxy.* El Cajon, CA: Zondervan.

Meyer, D. (1970). *The protestant search for political realism, 1919-1949.* Berkley, CA: Berkley University Press.

Morrow, L. (1981, May 11). What is the point of working? *Time.* Retrieved on April 2, 2006 from http://www.time.com/time/magazine/article/0,9171,949162,00.html

Myers, B. (nd). *Mission as transformation.* Oxford Centre for Mission Studies from http://www.ocms.ac.uk/regnum/detail.php?book_id=9.

Naisbitt, J. (1982). *Megatrends: Ten new directions transforming our lives.* New York, NY: Warner Books.

National Catholic War Council (1919, February 12). *Program of social reconstruction US bishops.* Washington, DC.

Niebuhr, R. (1920). The church and the industrial crisis. *Biblical World, 54*(6).

Noll, M. (2002). *The old religion in a new world.* Cambridge, UK: Wm. B. Eerdmans Publishing Company.

Novak, M. (1981). The economic system: The Evangelical basis of a social market economy. *Review of Politics, 43*(3).

Novak, M. (1993). *The Catholic ethic and the spirit of capitalism.* New York, NY: The Free Press.

Ohio Department of Job and Family Services Bureau of Labor Market Information/Office of Workforce Development (2004). *The graying of the Ohio labor force.* Columbus, OH: Ewald, K.

Penning, J. & Smidt, C. (2002). *Evangelicalism: The next generation.* Grand Rapids, MI: Baker Academic.

Philips, K. (2006). *American theocracy.* London, UK: Penguin Books.

Piderit, S. (1998). Out on a limb: The role of context and impression management in issue selling. *Administrative Science Quarterly, 43,* 23-57.

Poole, K., & Rosenthal (1997). *Congress. a political-economic history of roll call voting.* New York, NY: Oxford University Press.

Quinley, H. (1974). The dilemma of an activist church: Protestant religion in the sixties and seventies. *Journal for the Scientific Study of Religion, 13*(1).

Regnerus, M. & Smith, C. (1998). Selective deprivatization among American religious traditions: The reversal of the great reversal. *Social Forces, 76*(4).

Robinson, P. (1988). *The unbalanced recovery.* Oxford/New York: Philip Alan Publishers.

Rowthorn, R. & Ramaswamy, R. (1997). Deindustrialization: Causes and implications. Washington, DC: International Monetary Fund Asia and Pacific Department.

Russo, J. & Corbin, B. (1999, July/August). *Labor and the Catholic church: Opportunities for coalitions. Working USA, 3*(2), 9-89.

Russo, J. (2004, July). Worked over: The corporate sabotage of an American community. *Industrial & Labor Relations Review, 57*(4).

Safford, S. (2004). Why the garden club couldn't save Youngstown: Civic infrastructure and mobilization in economic crises. Cambridge, MA: Massachusetts Institute of Technology.

Saks, D. (1985). Dislocated Workers. *Society, 22*(4), 3.

Shuman, J. & Meador, K. (2003). *Heal thyself: Spirituality, medicine, and the distortion of Christianity.* New York, NY: Oxford University Press.

Somers, M. & Block, F. (2005). From poverty to perversity: ideas, markets, and institutions over 200 years of welfare debate. *American Sociological Review, 70*(2).

Stackhouse, M. (1984). *Creeds, society, and human rights: Study in three cultures.* Grand Rapids, MI: William Eerdman's Publishing Company.

Stand Up for Steel Archive (2006). Retrieved on September 3, 2006, from http://www.standupforsteel.com/archive.htm

Straub, J. (2006). What was the matter with Ohio? Unions and Evangelicals in the Rust Belt. *The Monthly Review, 57*(8). Retrieved March 23, 2006, from http://www.monthlyreview.org/0106straub.htm

Strenski, I. (2004). The religion in globalization. *Journal of the American Academy of Religion, 72*(3).

Suenens, L. & Camara, D. (1978). *Charismatic renewal and social action.* Cincinnati, OH: Servant Books.

Thomas, G. (1989). *Revivalism and cultural change.* Chicago, IL: University of Chicago Press.

Toffler, A. (1980). *The third wave.* New York, NY: Bantam Books.

Toffler, A. (1989). *Powershift.* New York, NY: Bantam Books.

Toffler, A. (1994). *Creating a new civilization.* Nashville, TN: Turner Publishing Company.

Toffler. A. (1995). Getting set for the coming millennium. *Futurist, 29*(2), 10.

Tournier, P. (1964). *The whole person in a broken world.* New York, NY: Harper & Row.

Trueblood, E. (1970). *The new man for our time.* New York, NY: Harper & Row.

US Bureau of Labor Statistics (2006). *Youngstown-Warren-Boardman, OH-PA.* Retrieved on July 15, 2006, from http://stats.bls.gov/eag/eag.oh_youngstown_msa.htm

US Department of Labor Bureau of Labor Statistics (2005). *NAICS 31-33: Manufacturing.* Retrieved on August 19, 2006, from http://www.bls.gov/iag/manufacturing.htm

Weber, M. (1958). *The protestant ethic and the spirit of capitalism.* New York, NY: Charles Scribner's Sons.

Weidenbaum, M. (2004, May). Smooth job transition to offset overseas outsourcing. USA Today. Retrieved on July, 2006, from http://findarticles.com/p/articles/mi_m1272/is_2708_132/ai_n6019796/

Witherington, B. (2005). *The problem with Evangelical theology.* Waco, TX: Baylor Press.

Youngstown Area Regional Chamber of Commerce (2006). *Educational Attainment/Labor Force Participation.* Retrieved on October 4, 2006, from http://www.regionalchamber.com/labor-educational.htm

(2006, April 6). Youngstown Vindicator.

(2006, August 19). Youngstown Vindicator.

(2006, June 14). Youngstown Vindicator.

(2006, June 27). Youngstown Vindicator.

(2006, June 8). Youngstown Vindicator.

(2006, November 11). Youngstown Vindicator.

(2006, November 4). Youngstown Vindicator.

(2006, November 4). Youngstown Vindicator.

(2006, September 4). Youngstown Vindicator.

Related Works

Argyle, M. (1989). *The social psychology of work.* London, UK: Penguin Books.

Baltzell, E. (1982), *Puritan Boston and Quaker Philadelphia.* Boston, MA: Beacon Press.

Behravesh, N. & Klein, L. (2004). Report prepared by Global Insight for the Information Technology Association of America: *The comprehensive impact of offshore it software and services outsourcing on the US economy and the IT industry.* Arlington, VA.

Catholic Bishops of the United States (1975). *The economy: Human dimension.* Washington, DC: United States Catholic Conference.

DeBerri, E. & Hug, J. (1985). *Catholic social teaching: Our best kept secret.* Maryknoll, NY: Obris Books.

Dombek, K. (1995). Shopping for the end of the world: 'Left behind', evangelical culture, and apocalyptic consumerists. (Doctoral dissertation, New York: New York State University, 2005).

Erikson, K. & Vallas, S. (1990). *The nature of work: Sociological perspectives.* New Haven, CT: Yale University Press.

Fishman, R. (1987). *Bourgeois utopias: The rise and fall of suburbia.* New York, NY: Basic Books.

Kugel, Y. & Gruenberg, G. (1977). *Ethical perspectives on business and society.* Lexington, MA: Lexington Books.

Lakoff, S. (1964). *Equality in political philosophy.* Cambridge, MA: Harvard University Press.

MacKinnon, B. (1998). *Ethics theory and contemporary issues: Second edition.* Belmont, CA: Wadsworth Publishing Company.

Mattox, R. (1978). *The Christian employee.* New Brunswick, NJ: Bridge-Logos Publishers.

McShane, J. (1986). *Sufficiently radical: Catholicism, progressivism, and the bishops programs of 1919.* Washington, DC: Catholic University of America Press.

Mehl, R. (1970). *Catholic ethics and protestant ethics.* Philadelphia, PA: Westminster Press.

Mueller, F. (1984). *The church and the social question.* Washington, DC: The American Enterprise Institute for Public Policy Research.

Novak, M. (1982). *The spirit of democratic capitalism.* New York, NY: Touchstone Publishing.

O'Brien Steinfels, M. (2004). *American Catholics and civic engagement: A distinctive voice.* Lanham, MD: Rowman & Littlefield Publishers.

Raab, E. & Selznick, J. (1964). *Major social problems.* New York, NY: Harper & Row.

Rauschenbusch, W. (1997). *A theology for the social gospel.* Louisville, KY: Westminster John Knox Press.

Rojek, C. (1985). *Capitalism and leisure theory.* London/New York: Tavistock Publications.

Ross, R. & Trachte, K. (1990). *Global capitalism: The new leviathan.* Albany, NY: State University of New York Press.

Schlossberg, H., Samuel, V., & Sider, R. (1994). *Christianity and economics in the post-cold war era: The Oxford declaration and beyond.* Grand Rapids, MI: William B. Eerdman's Publishing Company.

Schultz, S. (2005, December 28). Calls made to strengthen state energy policies. The Country Today, pp. 1A, 2A.

Sharlet, J. (1999). Seeking solidarity in the culture of the working class. *Chronicle of Higher Education, 45*(46).

Veblen, T. (1953). *The theory of the leisure class.* New York, NY: Mentor Books.

Volti, R. (1988). *Society and technological change.* New York, NY: St. Martin's Press.

Index

1960s, 48, 78
1977, 5, 6, 11, 18, 25, 27, 28, 29, 30, 35, 36, 50, 51, 53, 61, 62, 64, 67, 77, 91, 95, 96, 97, 98, 103, 104, 105, 106, 107, 108, 109, 110, 111, 113, 114, 115, 116, 117, 118, 133, 161
2007, 2, 11, 12, 18, 19, 27, 28, 29, 30, 60, 61, 63, 64, 67, 74, 77, 79, 91, 92, 95, 105, 108, 115, 116, 117, 119, 124
accountability, 58
activism, 21, 22, 25, 41, 46, 47, 48, 53, 79, 88, 92, 98, 110, 114, 135, 136
activist, 121, 122, 157
affluence, 62, 109
agrarian. *See* agriculture
agricultural. See agriculture, See agriculture, See agriculture, See agriculture, See agriculture
Allentown, 61
American, 12, 17, 18, 21, 31, 33, 34, 35, 39, 40, 41, 42, 43, 46, 48, 51, 58, 59, 60, 66, 67, 69, 70, 72, 77, 78, 80, 82, 84, 85, 86, 87, 89, 91, 99, 104, 123, 138, 152, 153, 154, 155, 157, 158, 159, 162
American Federation of Labor, 43, 58
assembly lines, 48
attitude, 82
baby-boomer, 20, 72
biblical, 114, 125, 128, 129, 139
bishops, 43, 49, 157, 162
blue-collar, 36, 57, 81, 96, 106
bureaucracy, 43
capitalism, 38, 39, 40, 43, 57, 60, 70, 79, 84, 112, 157, 159, 162
Catholic, 12, 27, 28, 31, 41, 42, 43, 45, 49, 51, 80, 83, 99, 113, 120, 124, 136, 157, 158, 161, 162
Catholic diocese, 51
Center for Working Class Studies, 12, 60, 74, 75
Chamber of Commerce, 71, 74, 160

Charismatic, 159
charity, 25, 43, 46, 82, 87, 88, 92, 97, 108, 109, 114, 137, 138, 139
church, 43, 47, 48, 52, 83, 90, 106, 109, 116, 120, 123, 124, 125, 127, 128, 130, 131, 133, 134, 155, 157, 158, 162
Church of the Locality, 7, 132
CIO, 58, 81
city-church, 133
civil rights, 78, 85
civilization, 40, 90, 127, 159
clergy, 6, 11, 20, 21, 22, 23, 25, 28, 29, 30, 42, 44, 47, 48, 50, 51, 54, 78, 83, 95, 96, 97, 98, 103, 104, 105, 106, 107, 108, 109, 110, 111, 112, 113, 114, 115, 116, 117, 118, 121, 122, 123, 132, 134, 135, 138, 139, 140
coalition. *See* Ecumenical Coalition
common good, 129
compassion, 43, 87
competitive, 61, 83, 90, 154

concept of the church of the region, 133
congregation, 106, 107, 109
Congress of Industrial Organizations, 58
conservative, 45, 77, 79, 81, 85, 154
consumer, 58, 59, 79
consumerism, 80, 81, 83, 84, 86, 88, 112, 138
consumers, 60, 83, 89
corporate, 11, 24, 53, 54, 58, 60, 64, 65, 70, 92, 104, 114, 116, 138, 139, 153, 158
crisis, 19, 20, 21, 23, 24, 29, 31, 50, 51, 52, 53, 62, 64, 66, 67, 77, 89, 104, 109, 111, 116, 154, 155, 157
culture, 34, 38, 79, 84, 91, 104, 112, 120, 126, 128, 132, 161, 162
decline, 18, 22, 28, 37, 62, 63, 68, 78, 96, 153
deindustrialization, 17, 24, 26, 28, 30, 41, 49, 50, 51, 58, 61, 88, 90, 91, 95, 98, 103, 104, 105, 106, 107,

108, 109, 110, 111, 114, 115, 116, 117, 123, 138, 139, 140
Delphi, 62, 64
denomination, 134
Department of Housing and Urban Development, 52
deskilled, 41
dialectic, 134, 135, 136, 137, 138
dialog, 113, 114, 117, 120, 138, 139
downsizing, 6, 20, 29, 59, 61, 64, 65, 72, 90, 92, 97, 104, 109, 110, 113, 114, 116, 138, 139
Drucker, Peter, 15
economic change, 105, 107
Economic Development Administration, 54
economic fallout, 75
economic growth, 16, 22, 43, 152
economic power, 53
economic theory, 50
Ecumenical Coalition, 5, 6, 11, 25, 28, 30, 50, 51, 52, 53, 55, 77, 91, 95, 96, 97, 98,
103, 104, 105, 106, 107, 108, 109, 110, 111, 112, 113, 114, 115, 116, 117, 118, 133
ecumenism, 12, 122, 123, 133
Education, 73, 162
entrepreneur, 83
Episcopal, 31, 51, 80, 100
ethical, 17, 40, 44, 55, 65
European, 41, 42
evangelicalism, 77, 78, 79, 80, 82, 83, 84, 85, 87, 88, 89, 127, 155, 156
Evangelicalism, 6, 79, 82, 84, 86, 88, 90, 91, 115, 123, 127, 155, 157
evil, 46, 155
exploitation, 44
extremes, 134
faith-based, 87
Focus on the Family, 87
Fourth Wave, 7, 93, 119, 120, 121, 123, 132, 138
free market, 70, 83, 84, 85, 86, 87, 88
free society, 88
Free Trade, 58, 69, 70

Fundamentalism, 127
Fundamentalist, 27, 28, 30, 78, 120, 136
future, 11, 23, 26, 29, 30, 50, 54, 55, 73, 92, 105, 113, 115, 117, 120, 126, 127, 136, 138, 153
General Motors Lordstown, 62
German, 47
God, 39, 40, 44, 45, 49, 81, 85, 86, 90, 99, 100, 125, 126, 127, 128, 129, 130, 131, 132, 135, 139, 152
gospel, 45, 46, 47, 48, 79, 82, 84, 85, 92, 125, 155, 162
government, 18, 43, 46, 53, 75, 104, 110, 114, 131, 133, 138, 156
higher education, 74
human rights, 42, 59, 71, 158
hypotheses, 28, 96, 100, 103, 104, 117
immigrant, 41, 42
import, 70
individual needs, 88
individualism, 25, 59, 79, 82, 83, 90, 92, 112

industrial, 15, 16, 18, 21, 22, 34, 35, 37, 38, 41, 43, 48, 51, 60, 69, 71, 78, 122, 155, 157
Industrial Revolution, 5, 33, 34, 38, 39, 40, 46
industrialism, 16, 18, 34, 38, 41, 42, 44, 46, 47, 57, 60, 113
industrialists. *See* industrialization
industrialization, 17, 34, 38, 40, 41, 44, 49, 50
injustice, 44, 53, 111, 114
interfaith, 52
Internet, 57, 105
Jesuits, 42
Jesus, 45, 53, 135, 154
jobs, 11, 20, 33, 34, 35, 36, 41, 42, 58, 61, 63, 64, 66, 67, 68, 69, 70, 71, 72, 78, 81, 138, 153, 155, 156
John Russo, 12, 60, 74
justice, 25, 41, 43, 44, 45, 46, 47, 48, 53, 58, 78, 84, 85, 88, 92, 96, 97, 106, 107, 108, 113, 123, 132, 136, 137, 138, 139
kingdom of God, 129, 130

Kruskal-Wallis, 100, 101, 103
labor, 16, 18, 19, 20, 21, 22, 23, 24, 29, 30, 33, 35, 37, 38, 39, 40, 41, 42, 43, 44, 49, 58, 59, 60, 61, 62, 63, 64, 66, 68, 69, 70, 71, 72, 73, 75, 77, 78, 80, 82, 90, 91, 104, 113, 116, 153, 157, 160
labor force, 21, 72
labor movement, 42
laissez-fair, 86
Lausanne Covenant, 7, 125, 126
layoffs, 19, 72, 74, 153
liberal, 46, 47, 48, 77, 78
low-skilled, 73
Mahoning Valley, 5, 18, 20, 25, 28, 29, 30, 36, 37, 50, 61, 62, 63, 64, 65, 74, 75, 77, 92, 95, 99, 133
Mainline, 5, 25, 27, 28, 31, 48, 49, 77, 78, 79, 83, 84, 85, 120, 121, 123, 127, 128, 135, 136, 139
Mainline Protestant. *See* mainline
Mann-Whitney U, 100, 101, 103

manufacturers, 18, 19, 36, 39, 65, 66
manufacturing, 20, 22, 23, 24, 29, 30, 36, 37, 39, 40, 49, 58, 59, 60, 62, 63, 64, 66, 67, 68, 69, 71, 72, 74, 77, 78, 79, 86, 92, 105, 108, 113, 116, 159
market discipline, 85, 88, 89
marketable, 73
marketplace ministry, 124, 127, 131, 132
materialism, 40, 85, 112
McKinsey Global Institute, 72, 156
megachurch, 85
middle-class, 20, 71, 86
Midwest, 35, 49
mission, 12, 20, 43, 46, 47, 123, 125, 128, 130
missional living, 127, 128, 130, 132
money, 85, 132
moral, 43, 44, 47, 53, 54, 86, 88, 89, 91, 92, 110
morality, 91, 110
moratorium, 70
Naisbitt, John, 15, 156

New Deal, 47, 81
nineteenth century, 41, 42, 46, 86
Northeast, 35, 49
obsolete, 34, 58
Ohio, 5, 18, 23, 29, 35, 36, 37, 61, 62, 64, 66, 70, 72, 73, 74, 81, 119, 153, 154, 157, 158
Organized labor, 58
Packard Electric, 62
paradigm, 58, 134
peace, 45, 85
Pennsylvania Manufacturer's Association, 66
per capita income, 61, 62
personal salvation, 85, 87
Philips, Kevin, 16, 17, 59, 78, 82, 87, 157
pietist, 121, 122
piety, 25, 82, 85, 88, 89, 90, 92, 97, 109, 114, 132, 137
Polarization, 122
policy, 24, 49, 71, 86, 133, 152
political, 11, 16, 21, 36, 43, 47, 48, 53, 59, 60, 78, 79, 86, 87, 89, 92, 112, 113, 115, 117, 120, 121, 122, 125, 129, 154, 155, 156, 157, 161
politicians, 71
politics, 52, 86, 89, 91, 152
poor, 39, 43, 45, 53, 71, 85, 124
Pope Leo XIII, 46
post-Christian, 132
Postmodernism, 120
Presbyterian Church, 31, 49, 52, 100
Presbyterians, 54, 78
Productivity, 33, 69, 152
profit, 39
progress, 15, 16, 17, 57, 60, 69, 92, 129, 154
progressive, 45, 124, 126
proselytize, 88, 132
protest, 48
Protestant Ethic, 38, 39, 46, 110, 132
public, 17, 19, 21, 24, 46, 49, 51, 53, 55, 77, 78, 79, 80, 89, 128, 131, 133
Puritan. *See* puritanical
puritanical, 39, 46, 136

quaternary sector, 119
quinary sector, 120
realism, 48, 129, 156
recession, 37
recovery, 19, 24, 29, 63, 105, 118, 120, 122, 123, 128, 133, 157
redemption, 44, 130
religion, 17, 21, 23, 24, 27, 28, 30, 41, 42, 44, 45, 46, 49, 51, 55, 59, 78, 79, 80, 82, 83, 84, 88, 89, 91, 93, 104, 108, 110, 111, 112, 113, 114, 122, 140, 153, 154, 155, 157, 159
Religious Attitudes Toward Deindustrialization, 96, 97, 98, 99
religious community, 18, 19, 20, 23, 29, 41, 44, 51, 52, 91, 108, 110, 112, 116, 117, 118, 120, 123, 133
religious leaders, 17, 21, 46, 52, 54, 55, 75
renewal, 24, 48, 120, 123, 129, 136, 140, 159
Republican, 81, 86, 89

research, 11, 12, 23, 24, 26, 28, 29, 30, 95, 98, 103, 104, 116, 117, 119, 120, 121, 122, 123, 134, 136, 137, 138, 140, 153, 155
responsibility, 17, 49, 58, 88, 90, 110, 111, 114, 115, 116
retraining, 74, 75, 116, 153
rich, 39, 45, 152
right-wing, 78, 81
rustbelt, 18, 19, 23, 29, 34, 55, 61, 91, 92, 104, 120
Second Wave, 5, 15, 16, 18, 19, 21, 22, 23, 25, 27, 28, 33, 34, 35, 37, 41, 42, 44, 46, 48, 50, 51, 53, 55, 57, 58, 59, 60, 61, 63, 68, 69, 71, 72, 73, 75, 77, 78, 79, 80, 82, 83, 84, 88, 89, 91, 92, 104, 105, 106, 108, 110, 111, 112, 113, 114, 115, 130, 136
self-reliance, 86, 110
shutdown, 25, 27, 36, 52
skill, 61, 73

social change, 17, 39, 114, 115, 120, 122, 127, 129, 136, 137
Social Christianity, 47
social divisions, 60
social evils, 47, 115
social gospel, 47, 48, 84
Social Gospel, 28, 47, 113, 127, 129, 136, 154
social justice. *See* justice
social problems, 48, 82, 88, 108, 115, 134, 162
social psychology, 39, 161
social reform, 87
social research, 23, 99
socialist, 46, 155
socioeconomic, 17, 18, 20, 24, 28, 30, 77, 86, 91, 92, 96, 104, 106, 107, 108, 112, 114, 115, 116, 134
socio-economic, 139
sociopolitical, 38, 52
socio-religious, 38, 82, 137
Stand Up for Steel, 66, 70, 158
steel, 18, 19, 21, 23, 25, 29, 31, 35, 36, 37, 50, 51, 52, 53, 54, 62, 63, 64, 66, 67, 69, 70, 77, 81, 154
steel mills, 18, 35, 50
steel production, 52
steel strike. *See* strike
Steel to Scholars, 75
strike, 35, 105
structural, 44, 110, 114, 115, 127, 136
suburban, 6, 63, 82, 97, 108, 109, 113, 114
suburbanization, 21, 62, 63, 82
synthesis, 127, 134, 135
technological shift, 57, 69
technology, 16, 18, 57, 60, 73, 74, 105, 112, 138, 152
tertiary sector, 119
theological, 11, 16, 42, 44, 48, 53, 84, 91, 104, 117, 120, 121, 122, 124, 125, 129, 134, 139
theology, 46, 47, 84, 88, 92, 116, 120, 123, 125, 127, 129, 135, 138, 160, 162
Third Wave, 5, 6, 11, 15, 16, 18, 21, 22, 23, 25, 26, 27, 28, 37, 49, 55, 57, 58, 59, 60, 61,

62, 63, 65, 66, 67, 68, 69, 70, 71, 72, 73, 74, 75, 77, 78, 79, 80, 82, 83, 84, 85, 86, 87, 88, 89, 90, 91, 92, 104, 105, 106, 107, 108, 110, 111, 112, 113, 115, 119, 120, 121, 122, 128, 137, 138
Toffler. *See* Toffler, Alvin
Toffler, Alvin, 5, 11, 15, 16, 24, 30
tradition, 17, 20, 80, 83, 136, 139
trans-denominational, 124
transformation, 11, 21, 29, 41, 61, 82, 105, 122, 124, 125, 126, 127, 130, 134, 135, 140, 156
transformational, 123, 125, 127, 128, 129, 131, 133, 135, 136
transformationalism, 120, 123, 124, 125, 127, 129, 132, 134, 137
transformative, 81
transition, 17, 18, 20, 21, 22, 37, 46, 59, 60, 61, 62, 68, 69, 70, 71, 72, 73, 74, 75, 82, 90, 92, 106, 113, 119, 121, 153, 159
trends, 15, 21, 24, 30, 60, 63, 66, 68, 72, 80, 138, 152
twentieth century, 35, 41, 48, 59, 77, 79, 106
tyranny, 43
unemployed. *See* unemployment
unemployment, 36, 49, 66, 67, 68, 152
unemployment insurance, 67
unions, 20, 42, 54, 58, 60, 64, 80, 81
United Church of Christ, 31, 49
United Methodist Church, 31, 49
United States, 2, 18, 21, 33, 35, 38, 40, 42, 43, 49, 52, 54, 57, 61, 66, 67, 68, 70, 72, 78, 119, 130, 161
United Steel Workers of America, 74
utopia, 129
Vatican II, 43
Victorian, 85
Vineyard, 125, 127
vocation, 39, 88
wages, 42, 65, 68, 116

Washington, 52, 54, 82, 156, 157, 158, 161, 162
wealth, 17, 38, 40, 46, 71
welfare, 42, 85, 87, 88, 116, 158
white-collar, 57, 96, 97, 106
work ethic, 40, 41, 88, 153
working class, 80, 84, 112, 162
working conditions, 42
World War, 34, 48
WYTV, 74
Youngstown, 5, 6, 11, 12, 18, 19, 20, 21, 22, 23, 24, 26, 28, 29, 30, 31, 33, 34, 35, 36, 37, 38, 50, 51, 52, 54, 55, 57, 58, 60, 61, 62, 63, 64, 65, 66, 67, 68, 69, 74, 75, 77, 79, 90, 91, 92, 96, 99, 103, 104, 105, 106, 107, 108, 110, 112, 113, 116, 117, 119, 120, 121, 122, 123, 126, 130, 133, 134, 135, 136, 138, 139, 140, 152, 154, 158, 159, 160
Youngstown Sheet and Tube, 36, 50, 62
Youngstown Vindicator, 65, 74, 90

www.ingramcontent.com/pod-product-compliance
Lightning Source LLC
Chambersburg PA
CBHW072135160426
43197CB00012B/2116